SCOTTISH ANTIQUES

Donald Wintersgill

JOHNSTON & BACON

LONDON & EDINBURGH

to my wife

A JOHNSTON & BACON book published by
CASSELL & COLLIER MACMILLAN PUBLISHERS LTD.
35 Red Lion Square, London WC1R 4SG
and Tanfield House, Tanfield Lane, Edinburgh EH3 5LL
and at Sydney, Auckland, Toronto, Johannesburg
an affiliate of
Macmillan Publishing Co.
New York

© Donald Wintersgill, 1977

First published 1977

ISBN 0 7179 4230 9

Filmset and printed in Great Britain by BAS Printers Limited, Over Wallop, Hampshire

Contents

STUARTS AND JACOBITES

THE ARTS

BALMORALITY—the Victorian View of Scotland

Preface

An educated non-Scot once told me that he did not think Scotland ever had her own coins. And many Scots, too, are little aware of their own remarkable heritage—remarkable because the nation's history is lurid with wars against the English and between Scots themselves; and because the country was often comparatively poor.

This book ranges wide in its subjects; and I have avoided a narrow definition of what is Scottish.

Scottish antiques are found not only in their native land. Like the Scots themselves they seem fond of travelling forth. They are in Britain as a whole; they often turn up in great London salerooms; they are collected in some instances all over the world, and especially where Scots have gone.

This is the first book to cover the field generally, although much has been written about specialised subjects, and of course I am much indebted to these works of research and scholarship. My hope is that this book will encourage all kinds of people to look afresh at what Scotland has produced; and that it will give the Scots themselves a better understanding of their history and heritage.

Donald Wintersgill
December 1976

Acknowledgements

The author wishes to thank, for their generous help in the preparation of this book:

Mr Francis Bamford; Mr Claude Blair, Keeper of Metalwork, Victoria and Albert Museum; Mr Brian Blench, Keeper of Decorative Art, Glasgow Art Gallery and Museum; Miss Sue Bond of Sotheby's; Mr David Bruce; Mr D J Bryden of the Whipple Museum of the History of Science, Cambridge; Mrs Shirley Bury of the Victoria and Albert Museum; Mr Stanley Clark, of Sotheby's and Clark Nelson Ltd; Mr Patrick Finn, of Spink and Son; Miss Fiona Ford, of Sotheby's; Mr Phillipe Garner, of Sotheby's Belgravia; Mr John Herbert, of Christie's; Mrs G E P How, of How of Edinburgh; Mr David S Howard, of Heirloom and Howard; Mr Andrew Hutton, of Spink and Son; Mr E C Joslin, of Spink and Son; Mr Edmund Laird-Clowes, of Spink and Son; Mr David Learmont, National Trust for Scotland; Dr Rosalind Marshall, of the Scottish National Portrait Gallery; Mr Stuart Maxwell, Deputy Director, National Museum of Antiquities of Scotland; Mr Colin Narbeth, of Stanley Gibbons; Mr Frank Purvey, of B A Seaby; Mrs Susan Rose, of Christie's; Mr George Schopflin; Mrs May Sinclair, of Spink and Son; Dr Alistair G Thomson, Keeper of Technology, Royal Scottish Museum; Mr W A Thorburn, Keeper, Scottish United Services Museum; Mr John Wallace; and Mr Peter Preston, Editor of the *Guardian*, for permission to use certain material from the paper. The author would also like to thank the curators of museums and historic houses who have supplied information. His especial thanks are given to Mr Maxwell.

Illustrations

Sotheby's and Christie's generously provided photographs from their archives, and this is indicated in the appropriate captions. Other photographs have been kindly lent by:

Asprey's—Cockpen chairs: Birmingham Museum and Art Gallery—Mauchline ware: Delomosne and Son—Jacobite glasses: John Dewar and Sons—'Monarch of the Glen' by Landseer (on jacket): Edinburgh Public Library—Hill and Adamson photograph of Dr Knox: Stanley Gibbons—bank notes (including bank note on jacket): Glasgow Archaeological Society—armourers' marks, from 'Notes on Swords with Signed Basket Hilts by Glasgow and Stirling Makers', by Whitelaw, *Transactions*, New Series, vol VIII, part IV: Glasgow Museums and Art Galleries—ceramics, pair of pistols (on jacket): Glasgow University—chair by Charles Rennie Mackintosh (on jacket): Her Majesty's Stationery Office—Regalia, long gun: How of Edinburgh—quaich: National Library of Scotland—Hill and Adamson photograph of Robert Adamson: National Museum of Antiquities of Scotland—arms, pewter touch plate, brooches and other jewellery: Private collection—snuff mull (on jacket): Royal Commission on the Ancient and Historical Monuments of Scotland—grave slab of Murchardus MacDuffie: Royal Scottish Museum—clocks, watches and scientific instruments: Scottish National Portrait Gallery—Tassie medallions, Hill and Adamson photographs, portrait of Highland Chief by Michael Wright (on jacket): Scottish Tourist Board—Balmoral Castle: B A Seaby—coins and tokens: Sotheby's—communion cups (on jacket): Spink and Son—commemorative medals, communion tokens, insignia of the Order of the Thistle, silver, snuff mull by William Jameson of Aberdeen, £20 piece of James VI (on jacket): the photograph of the Glasgow School of Art is by Mr Dennis Conway: certain of the colour photographs on the jacket are from the Cooper-Bridgeman Library.

Extracts quoted: the extract from *A History of the Scottish People* by T C Smout is given by permission of the publishers, William Collins Sons and Co. Ltd.: the extract from *Sublime Tobacco* by Compton Mackenzie is given by permission of the Society of Authors as the literary representative of the Estate of Compton Mackenzie.

Scotland

Wick

Stornoway

Tain

Elgin

Culloden

Inverness

Peterhead

Aberdeen

Balmoral

Dunottar

Laurencekirk

Montrose

Alyth

Arbroath

Scone

Perth

St. Andrews

Doune

Kirkcaldy

Pittenweem

Stirling

Dunbar

Greenock

Edinburgh

Prestonpans

Portobello

Berwick

Glasgow

Pollokshaws

Mauchline

Roxburgh

Ayr

ARMS AND ARMOUR

Swords and Dirks

The killing of foes and the slicing of victuals

Disorder lingered on in Scotland for far longer than in England. The last major pitched battle between two clans was in 1680 between the Sinclairs and the Breadalbane Campbells at Altimarlich, Caithness, and a traveller recorded in 1689 about the Highlanders:

Once or twice a year, great numbers of 'em get together and make a great descent into the Low-lands, where they plunder the inhabitants and so return back and disperse themselves. And this they are apt to do in the profoundest sense, it being not only natural to 'em to delight in rapine, but they do it on a kind of principle and in conformity to the prejudice they continually have to the Lowlanders, whom they generally take for so many enemies.

And in the Lowlands:

This country has always swarmed with such numbers of idle vagabonds as no laws could ever restrain . . . they are not only a most unspeakable oppression to poor tenants (who if they give not bread or some kind of provision to perhaps forty such villains a day are sure to be insulted by them) but they rob many poor people who live in houses distant from any neighbourhood.

Every able-bodied Highlandman had to carry arms in times of trouble—sword, targe or shield, dirk or dagger, or pistols. His weapons were distinct from the Lowlander's weapons until after the '45, when the martial tradition swiftly faded. Some of the tradition was, however, carried on by the Scottish regiments, which have served the United Kingdom well: the relics can still be seen in modern forms of military swords.

John Hume, who was captured by the Highlanders at the Battle of Falkirk (1746) wrote in his *History of the Rebellion in the Year 1745* that the Highlanders 'always appeared like warriors; as if their arms had been limbs and members of their bodies they were never seen without them; they travelled, they attended fairs and markets, nay they went to church with their broadswords and dirks; and in later times, with their muskets and pistols'.

The Government passed laws after the '15 and the '45—the Disarming Acts—to suppress the warlike tendency of the Scots, and especially the Highlanders.

Cash was offered for arms handed in, although many of these arms turned out to be obsolete or useless. Early Disarming Acts were partly ineffective: for

A grave slab showing a 'true' claymore. The slab, 5 feet 9 inches (175.2 cm) long, is at Oronsay Priory, Argyllshire, and was for the grave of Murchardus MacDuffie who died in 1539.

Top:
Sword by Walter Allan of Stirling, made between about 1735 and 1760: a superb piece of design. Allan transformed the classic broadsword hilts into works of art.

Above:
A basket-hilted sword mounted in silver and inscribed: 'Presented to Lieut. A K Gillespie, the Black Watch (Royal Highlanders) on his coming of age. Newton-le-Willows, 23rd March, 1886.' The silver hilt is pierced and engraved with thistles; the silver scabbard is also engraved with thistles. Sold by Christie's in 1972 for £399.

example, Highland gentlemen who went to the annual fair at Crieff were reported in about 1720 to have 'a poinard, knife and fork in one sheath hanging at the side of their belt, their pistol at the other and their snuff mull before, with a great broadsword at their side'.

Armed men such as these were a threat to the peace. General Wade, who helped to pacify the remoter parts of the country by building roads, issued 230 licences in 1725 allowing the carrying of gun, sword, and pistol by 'the forresters, drovers, and dealers in cattle and other merchandise belonging to the several Clans who have surrendered their arms'. The Disarming Acts after the '45 were more stringently enforced.

Swords

The word claymore can mean two entirely different kinds of weapon. (The word is from the Gaelic *claidheamh-mor*, i.e. great sword.) The first is the 'true claymore', which was a favourite in the sixteenth century. It is large and designed to whack or slash the opponent.

The guards or quillons are at an angle to the blade and are diamond-shaped in section. Each quillon ends in an ornament made of four open circles of iron.

Weapons of such age are rare. Many must have been broken up for scrap when they went out of fashion or became worn and rusty. Others were converted into more fashionble types. Yet a fair number—even a surprising number—survive. The theory is that the survivors were used as 'bearing swords', that is they were carried point upwards in front of a chief or noble as civic swords are sometimes borne today in front of a civic dignitary.

'True' claymores are depicted on carved stone slabs which were put on the graves of important people in the West Highlands and Islands.

The other sort of claymore has a steel cage or 'basket' round the hilt. Full armour for fighting men went out of use as firearms became more lethal and more common. A swordsman's hand was no longer protected by a steel gauntlet; so the basket-hilt sword was devised instead. And it was designed for both slashing and thrusting. A slash from the whole length of such a weapon could inflict a frightful wound, for example almost severing a shoulder. Basket-hilt swords were associated with the Scots and especially with the Highlanders by about 1600. Great art and ingenuity were sometimes shown in the design of the open-work basket.

Several sorts of craftsmen were needed to make a sword—armourers, gairdmakers, cutlers, and lorimers (workers in small objects of metal such as spurs and bridles). But some families in the Highlands were hereditary armourers to chiefs and held land in return.

Basket-hilted swords are now called broadswords if the blade has two edges and backswords if the blade has one edge. Many blades were imported, for example from Passau and Solingen, Germany; and some have inscribed on them 'GOTT BEWAHR DIE OPRECHTE SCHOTTEN' (God protect the honest Scots).

Many have the name Andrea Ferrara, which has fathered a curious story. Ferrara (the word has several spellings) was alleged to be a clever Spanish sword-smith who caught an apprentice spying on his secrets and killed him. Ferrara had to flee, arrived in Scotland, set up a workshop, and was connected with the court of James VI.

The story, delightful as it is, has not much truth in it, if any. Almost all Ferrara blades are German and of the seventeenth century or the eighteenth. It is true that a Ferrara was making swords in Venice in the sixteenth century. Perhaps one of his blades found its way to Scotland and was admired and the name was taken up as a sign of quality.

Some basket-hilt swords are not Scottish but were made for English regiments in the middle of the eighteenth century.

Dirks

The dirk was a Highland weapon. A brawl in Inverness in 1557 brought a man named Mans McGillmichell into court for 'the wranguse drawin of ane dowrk to Andro Dempster, and briking of the dowrk at the same Androis head'. A traveller in the Highlands in about 1617, Richard James, wrote of the Highlanders: 'The weapons which they use are a longe basket hilt sword, and long kind of dagger broad in the back and sharp at ye pointe which they call a durke.'

The sheaths often had pockets for a smaller knife, or a knife and fork, or a pair of knives. These show that the dirk was carried about at many occasions; they were for all sorts of purposes from the slicing of victuals to the killing of foes.

Blades were not always specially made, for the craftsmen did re-use blades from swords which were out of date or broken. The reason may have been thrift; or the better quality of German blades.

Hilts changed over the years. Early examples are cylindrical and are of wood, horn, or brass but wood became the commonest material. The full flowering of the hilt was from about 1700. Deep carving of interlaced lines and studs gave both beauty and a strong grip; this was a revival of the Celtic tradition of ornament.

Decline set in after the '45. Hilts took on a bulbous outline; studs of silver or brass became a fashion; the weapon became almost exclusively for the army. And

A classic dirk of about 1790 with its sheath, knife, and fork. The interlaced carving on the hilts is well done and attractive. The tapering of the blade is typical; the mounts are brass; the length of the dirk is just over 18 inches (45.7 cm).

Top:
A dirk of the Gordon Highlanders mounted in silver
and set with a cairngorm. The blade is 12½ inches
(31.8 cm) long; the silver has the Edinburgh
hallmark for 1919; the dirk was sold at Christie's
in 1972 for £241.50.

Above:
A Victorian dirk mounted in silver and made in
London; the blade is 14 inches (36 cm) long. Sold
at Christie's in 1972 for £168.

from about 1800 a further change took place. The hilt took on a decorative but far from martial thistle shape. Semi-precious stones or paste jewels appeared. Carving on the hilt degenerated. The dirk had become, in the words of the leading authority Mr John Wallace, a mere adjunct to Highland dress. An example of the long way that the dirk had travelled is one inscribed: 'To I. L. Pritchard, Esq., of the Theatre Royal, Edinr., from his friends Jas Blair and Rt Baird in admiration of his genius and character. Glasgow, May 17th 1828.'

The *sgian dubh* or *skene dhu* (Gaelic for black knife, i.e. black-hilted) is now worn in the top of the stocking, with the top sticking out and generally ornamented with a semi-precious stone or coloured glass. This custom seems to have started in the late eighteenth century. A slightly more sinister knife was hidden in the same way as spies and secret agents are said to do with hand guns, for an account written in 1737 says that some Highlanders 'carry a sort of knife which they call *skeen-ochles*, from its being concealed in the sleeve near the arm-pit'.

Targes

. . . or targets, for defence

Targes, the round shields of the Highlander, were necessary in violent times. John Williamson, a skinner in Inverness, had a quarrel in an alehouse with Murdo Mackay in October 1621; he took his 'suord and tairge', says an account of the time, followed Mackay, and struck him 'quherof he departed this present lyif immediatlie'. A Banffshire laird was at supper in 1634 when he was told that an outlawed man wanted to speak with him. He went forth 'with his sword and his targe in his hand' but was ambushed by the outlaw's men.

The typical targe—or, more correctly, target—was about 20 inches (48 cm) across and weighed between 4½ lb (2 kg) and 8 lb (3½ kg). It was made of two layers of oak or fir pegged together; the grain of one layer crossing the grain of the other to give strength. Total thickness was about ½ inch (1.2 cm). Cowhide

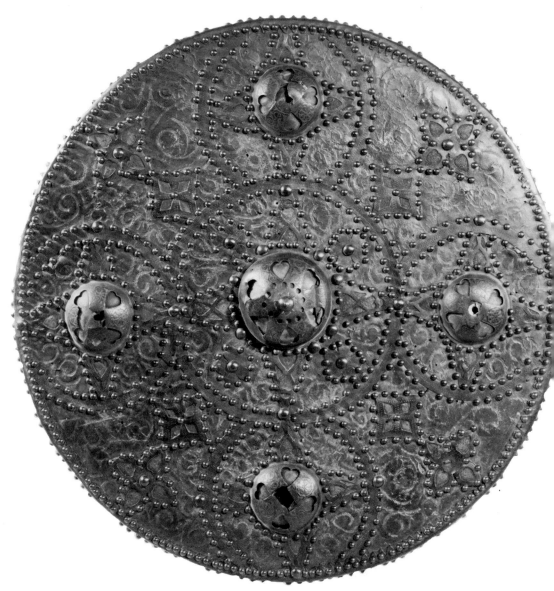

A fine and rare targe of wood, covered with tooled leather, studded with brass nail heads, and with bosses and plates of brass. The plates are pierced and some have red cloth beneath them. The bosses are pierced to reveal pieces of horn. It is 19½ inches (49.6 cm) across.

The central boss has concealed beneath it a brass plate engraved 'WF Invernes 1716.' This was revealed after the targe was sold at Christie's in 1972 for £661.50.

covered the front and hide, deerskin, or goatskin the back. A targe was a tough and handy thing, even able to give protection against a bullet.

The leather of the front was sometimes richly tooled with animals, birds, leaves, star shapes, panels, scrolls, or abstract patterns. Brass studs—and, rarely, silver studs—also formed patterns. Sometimes brass plates were added; and these sometimes are pierced and have red cloth behind them, which adds an attractive splash of colour.

Almost all have a central boss of brass which may have a hole to take a spike of steel. A targe of the Stewarts of Ardvorlich has a spike $11\frac{1}{2}$ inches (27.6 cm) long: an extra weapon against an adversary.

On the back was a loop of leather to put the arm through, a grip for the hand, and straps so that the targe could be slung over the user's back for easy carrying.

The ornamented targes were for the wealthy and simpler ones for the poor but very few have survived. Murray of Broughton was preparing in 1742 for the Rising that was to come and later wrote: 'The use of the Target had been long neglected . . . and though the materials might easily be found, it was difficult to procure a number of hands acquainted with their construction'. The Jacobite army was supplied in Perth and Edinburgh with targes which cost about five shillings each, the price of two pairs of shoes; better targes for the officers cost ten shillings.

The usefulness of the targe is shown by a story of an incident at the Battle of Killiecrankie in 1689. A Highlander and an English soldier were fighting with swords 'but the Scotchman received all the blows on his Target; and yet at the same time laid so hard at his Antagonist with his Broadsword that he cut him in two or three places; at which the Englishman enraged, rather than discouraged, cried out to him: "You Dog come out from behind the Door, and fight like a man!" '

Pacification of the Highlands after the '45 meant that targes were no longer needed or made. Many must have perished when the Government sought out and destroyed the Highlander's weapons. James Boswell said in 1773: 'There is hardly a target now to be found in the Highlands. After the disarming act they made them serve as covers to their buttermilk barrels, a kind of change like beating spears into pruning hooks'. Reproductions are now made to ornament the walls of cocktail lounges.

Pistols and Guns
Horns, fishtails, lemons, hearts and lobes

Scottish pistols were made in a unique and individual way in the eighteenth century. The classic form is entirely of steel or more rarely of brass; it is elegant in shape and decoration; the best specimens have fine silver inlay and engraved Celtic designs. The butt ends in two scrolling shapes like horns. No comprehensive collection of firearms is complete without a Scottish pistol or a pair of them; but they do tend to be expensive.

Scroll or ramshorn butt pistols were made from about the middle of the seventeenth century to the middle of the nineteenth. But the early ones are so scarce that they are museum pieces. The late ones are Scottish in appearance but were made in London or Birmingham and are thoroughly debased.

Pistols seem to have been worn on the left, hooked into a belt; or sometimes under the left armpit on a special shoulder-belt. All Scottish pistols have belt hooks and none have trigger guards. Most later ones have a 'pricker' or round-headed spike screwed into the butt; it was for cleaning the touch-hole.

Sporting rifle: the barrel is dated 1667 and the lock (the mechanism between the trigger and the gunpowder) is dated 1671. An outstanding and very rare gun. It was in the armoury of the Seafield family which was acquired by the nation in 1976.

Highlanders may have used these weapons more than Lowlanders did. Defoe wrote, in an outburst of prejudice, about the Highlanders in the early 1700's: 'They are all gentlemen, will take affront from no man, and insolent to the last degree. But certainly the absurdity is ridiculous to see a man in his mountain habit, armed with a broadsword, target, pistoll, at his girdle a dagger, and staff, walking down the High Street [of Edinburgh] as if he were a lord and withal driving a cow'.

It is likely that few pistols were made in the Highlands but rather in the towns such as Edinburgh, Glasgow, and Dundee and later in towns and villages along the edge of the Highlands. Of these the most famous was the village of Doune in south Perthsire. The great makers there were the families of Murdochs, Christies, Campbells, and Cadells. A pair by John Murdoch is said to have fired the first shots of the American War of Independence at the Battle of Lexington.

The industry in Dundee seems to have been almost destroyed when Cromwell's troops sacked the city in 1651. From that time Scottish firearms went their own way and were no longer influenced by the rest of Europe.

Another grave blow was the Proscription Act of 1746, which aimed to end for ever the threat of rebellion in Scotland. It forbade the Highlanders to wear their traditional dress and to carry arms. (The Privy Council had tried something similar in 1567: it issued an Act banning, on pain of death, the ownership by a civilian not needing firearms for state service the ownership of 'culveringis daggis pistolettis and uther sic ingynis of fyrewerk' because the use of them had caused men to be 'cowartlie and schaemfullie murtherit and slane'.) Attempts by the Government to disarm the Highlands after the risings of 1715 and 1745 must have meant the destruction of many arms; but pistols were comparatively easy to hide and so more of them seem to have survived.

The Highlands' social life and economy, after the '45, went through drastic changes; the Lowlands came more and more under English influence. Some of the workers in Doune migrated to other places. What saved the craft to some extent was the special status of the Scottish regiments. Officers and men were equipped with pistols of the traditional form—the men until 1795 and the officers in some regiments until the 1860s. But the army issue pistols were mass produced in Birmingham and were of very poor quality.

The Proscription Act was repealed in 1782 and the gunsmiths did produce some good pistols for individuals and some very fine ones for presentation. The *Statistical Account of Scotland* of 1798, a review of the state of the nation, said of Doune: 'There is now very little demand for Scottish pistols, owing to the low price of pistols made in England; but the chief cause of the decline is the disuse of the dirk and pistol as part of the Caledonian dress; and when Mr Murdoch gives over business, the trade, in all probability, will become extinct.' The prophecy came true.

Sir Walter Scott's novels brought about a romantic revival of Highland dress. It was reinforced by the State visit of George IV to Edinburgh in 1822—the King wore a kilt but with flesh-coloured tights so that the royal knees would not be exposed to the vulgar gaze.

This slightly comic interlude contrasts with incidents in the lives of George IV's ancestors. James II of Scotland was killed in 1460 by the bursting of a gun during a siege of Roxburgh. Emissaries from Henry VIII of England had difficulty in gaining access to James IV in April 1508 because he was experimenting with the manufacture of gunpowder. James IV, who was probably the founder of the firearms industry in Scotland, held shooting contests with his friends in which he lost bets. He also had to compensate the owner of a cow that was accidentally shot.

Pistols after the early nineteenth century were made in London or Birmingham. A leading authority on arms and armour, Mr Claude Blair, has written that the most elaborate examples were 'grossly over-decorated with cairngorms, thistles, stags, and all the worst features of what can only be described as Victorian Scottish rococo'. They are of interest only as examples of taste.

The other forms of pistols are rare and are likely to be in museums or the collections of the rich. They are classified according to the shape of the butt.

Fishtail butt: developed by the end of the sixteenth century, and also found in English pistols. The end has three lobes rather like a fish's tail. Scotland was exporting pistols to England in 1589 and 1597 and the English specimens may be copies. Most have stocks of Brazil wood (*Guilandina echinata*), a red wood very popular in Scotland until 1650 for the stocks of firearms—i.e. the part behind the lock mechanism. This type of pistol died out around 1625.

Lemon butt: a version of a type used all over Europe in the late sixteenth and early seventeenth centuries. The end is in the shape of an oval. It was made roughly at the same time as the fishtail butt. Both kinds of pistols have characteristically Scottish barrels: the muzzles are flared and separated from the barrels by a moulding or an inlaid band.

A gap of about 30 years interrupts the history of Scottish pistols, perhaps because of the civil strife that lasted from 1638 to 1651. Mr Blair says: 'The firearms produced subsequently are much less sophisticated and much further away from the mainstream of European development, and much more a part of Scottish folk art than those belonging to the earlier period. Their decoration, which was always engraved, often on inlaid bands and panels of silver, was now normally almost entirely Celtic in its inspiration, involving such motifs as knotted strapwork, trumpet scrolls, and the swastika—a fact that probably points to production having spread away from the old centres to workshops along the Highland Line'. These later pistols are—

Heart butt: The end of the butt is shaped like a heart with the point uppermost and seems to be a development of the lemon butt. It lasted from about 1660 to about 1730. Most are entirely of steel.

Lobe butt: Like the classic Highland pistol except that the butt is circular in cross-section and ends in a lobe-like dome. It seems to have been made only in the late eighteenth century. Perhaps this type was designed to be more like ordinary English pistols of the time and thus to be more saleable in the Lowlands. They are rare. A pair made by Thomas Murdoch was bequeathed by Washington to Lafayette and was described as being 'taken from the enemy'.

Examples of Scottish pistols turn up not only in Britain but also in other countries. They may have been taken abroad by travellers, emigrants, or

A pair of all-steel flintlock pistols made by J Murdoch of Doune about 1750 to 1775. They are engraved with scrolling foliage and the butts are inlaid with silver. The 'ram's horn' end of the butts is typical of the classic Scottish pistol. This pair, 10¾ inches (27.3 cm) long, was sold at Christie's in 1975 for £1963.

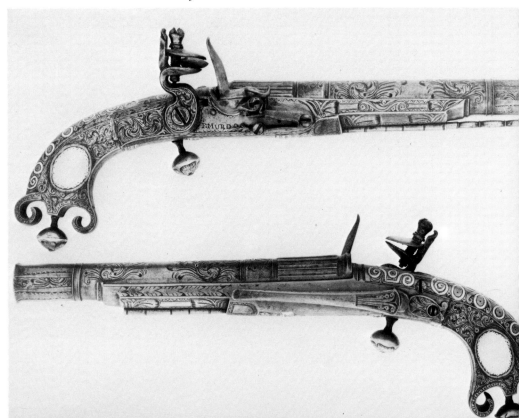

Armourers' marks. Left, John Simpson, senior, of Glasgow (late seventeenth century and early eighteenth). Centre, John Simpson the younger, his son (first half of eighteenth century). Right, Walter Allan, who became a freeman of the Incorporation of Hammermen of Stirling in 1732.

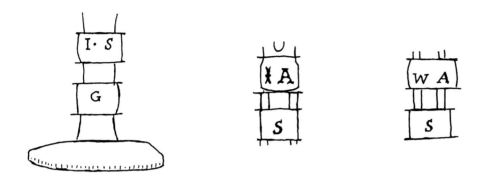

mercenaries, just as snuff mulls were. Collectors are international too, but owners often are reluctant to sell.

Condition is always important for a pistol's desirability and value but many examples have survived well because people have cherished them. Damp and rust were the implacable enemies. Dating a specimen is difficult sometimes: the classical type varied little in the eighteenth century. The frugal Scots, too, commonly 'cannibalised' bits and pieces of old guns in the making of new.

Fakes and forgeries of all-steel pistols are about. Some were made by Robert Glenn (1835–1911), a bagpipe maker of Edinburgh who seems to have been a highly skilled craftsman. More fakes have been made since the Second World War.

Guns

The earliest known firearms are four gun-barrels of the late sixteenth century. Three of them show high standards of workmanship. But 'long guns'—weapons longer than a pistol—are rare. Many must have been destroyed after the '15 and the '45. Only 28 are known to have survived and 13 are from the family armoury of the Earls of Seafield. This collection was acquired by the nation in lieu of death duties in 1976.

Documents and illustrations are few. Styles of guns did not change much over the years; parts of old guns were 'cannibalised' to make new, as has been mentioned in the section about pistols. Makers did not sign their work until towards the end of the seventeenth century; until then they normally put on their initials and more than one gunmaker had the same initials.

Brazil wood was popular for the stocks (see the section on fishtail butt pistols). True Scottish long guns have a special form of stock: the upper edge is concave, the lower is convex; and the sides are flat.

The Percussion Gun

A better way to shoot ducks and others

The father of the modern gun was an unlikely person: the craggy-faced Reverend Alexander Forsyth, (1768–1843) minister of Belhelvie, which is about eight miles north of Aberdeen. He was a great experimental scientist, had sound business sense, and struggled tenaciously against daunting difficulties. He was also a diligent and loved pastor for 52 years.

The difficulties he faced were daunting indeed: jealousy from gunmakers, 'pirates' who infringed his patent rights, bad debts, shortage of capital, niggardliness by the Government, untrustworthy workmen, and reluctance by the public to adopt his invention.

The invention was a better way to ignite the charge of gunpowder in guns; and he modified, for this new system, the 'lock' or the mechanism of a gun between the trigger and the charge. For generations the gunpowder had been set off by a flint striking steel and making a spark: the flintlock method. His invention was to set off the charge by a hammer striking a volatile substance and setting off a tiny explosion: the percussion method. It was rather like what happens when a hammer hits a match head. The advantage was ease and reliability in shooting and less trouble from damp getting into the works. A report about an incident in the Opium War with China in 1841 said: 'A company of Sepoys, armed with flint lock muskets which would not go off in heavy rain, were closely surrounded by some one thousand Chinese and were in some imminent peril, when two companies of Marines armed with percussion cap muskets were ordered up, and soon dispersed the enemy with great loss'.

Forsyth's father was minister of Belhelvie and the future inventor went when he was thirteen years old to King's College, one of the two universities in Aberdeen (they are now united). He took his Master of Arts degree in 1786 and went on to study divinity. His father died in 1790 and the young man succeeded him as minister of Belhelvie soon after.

Forsyth had a workshop in a wood about 50 yards from the manse; it was called the 'minister's smiddy' (smithy). There he conducted experiments in volatile compounds such as the fulminates of mercury and silver. Curious stories about him were later part of the family's tradition: that an explosion once blew him out of the smiddy and that a pet goose followed the minister as he strode up and down the avenue of the manse and pondered his sermons. If he was absent an old servant, the story goes, would say: 'Och, he's awa' at the shore, thinkin' aboot his guns, and his locks, and his thingies, and he'll jest be back wi' weet feet, for he never looks when the sea's comin' up'.

Another story is that he was shooting wildfowl on a loch when he noticed that many birds saw the flash from his flintlock gun, dived, and escaped the shot. The flint on flintlock arms generally strikes a spark into a small amount of powder— 'priming powder'—in a small hollow just below the touch hole. The priming powder burns for a split second before the flame actually gets through the hole

The Rev Dr Alexander Forsyth, inventor.

and sets fire to the main charge of powder in the barrel. There is thus a distinct lag between the first flash of the priming powder and the discharge of the gun. It is said that Forsyth covered the lock with a hood to hide the flash; a device made unnecessary by the percussion lock. With the percussion system the fire from the detonating compound goes straight into the main charge of powder and does not give a warning flash.

Forsyth went off to London in 1806 with his freshly developed invention. The Master General of the Ordnance, Lord Moira, arranged for Forsyth to be given workmen and facilities at the Tower of London for more experiments. The Tower was then the national arsenal.

Lord Moira promised that his expenses would be met by the Government and that he would get a reward. Forsyth estimated that the percussion lock would save about a seventh of the gunpowder used in flintlock weapons. He and Lord Moira agreed that the reward should be the value of the amount of gunpowder the army saved in two years, if the army adopted the percussion method.

Forsyth went ahead with his work, later renting a workshop outside the Tower because the workmen there became too inquisitive about what was going on. But the experiments ran into snags, a different Master General of the Ordnance was appointed, and the arrangements between the Government and Forsyth were ended. He was paid expenses and went back to Belhelvie.

Forsyth did, however, patent his invention, with the help of his friend James Watt, the engineer. He set up a gunmaking business with his cousin James Brougham who put up capital. (James Brougham's brother Henry became Lord Chancellor and gave his name to the carriage called a brougham). The firm, Forsyth and Co., was a perpetual worry from its setting up in 1808 until it was sold in 1819 to the manager; it survived until 1852. Forsyth and Brougham decided that their firearms would be of the very best quality and their shop would be in one of the most fashionable parts of London. All that cost a lot.

A campaign of words was carried on against the invention by the other gunmakers, who were jealous and afraid. This happened, for example, when

General Sir James Pulteney, Bart., who had an income of £50,000 a year by the will of his late wife the Countess of Bath, was badly wounded by an explosion when he was shooting: his left eye was blown out and he died six days later. One account of the accident blamed his gun's lock, made by Forsyth and Co. Another account blamed his flask of powder, 'made of the oxygenated muriate of potash (the priming powder for Forsyth locks,) which takes fire from the slightest blow or even friction'.

These reports were gravely damaging to the firm, which wrote to the *Sporting Magazine*: 'The gun . . . from its absolutely perfect state proves that it could not have undergone any explosion in its lock.' The flask had contained common gunpowder and Forsyth's priming powder 'is incapable of spontaneous explosion, even if Sir James had had any with him at the time'.

Gunmakers may have spread alarm about the Forsyth products but were willing to pirate the invention. The result was costly law suits against the pirates, which Forsyth and Co. won. Brougham was so hard pressed by his creditors in 1817 that he was thinking of selling the business. The business itself was short of cash and Forsyth wrote to Brougham in 1819, 'I hope that . . . the great English gentry who drive about in their carriages through London, Bath, etcetera, will think that it is decent, I shall not say honest, to pay tradesmen's acounts'.

Odds against the firm were too great: Forsyth was hundreds of miles away and Brougham was hard up and wanted to spend more time in politics. The two men sold the firm to Charles Uther, who had been a partner for some years. The rest of its history is undistinguished.

Forsyth's invention was praised as early as 1814 in *Instructions to Young Sportsmen*: 'If a man is so destitute of resource within himself, as to be miserable unless he is shooting, he has only to provide himself with one of Mr Forsyth's fulminating locks, which certainly will defy the weather longer than any other; though perhaps from the strong acid produced by the powder, they may not be proof against a continual pour of rain. The invention is certainly of infinite merit'.

Twenty-five years later, in 1839, the army got round to issuing percussion

A 14-bore sporting gun by Forsyth and Co, 28 inches (71 cm) long. The lock plate is engraved with ducks and a dog. It was made in 1810 and was sold at Christie's in 1974 for £819.

muskets to some of the troops. Forsyth had been made an honorary Doctor of Laws by King's College, Aberdeen, in 1834; and in the same year he began a campaign for the Government to give him better financial recognition of his work. This campaign was to end only with his death in 1843. He enlisted the help of Lord Brougham, of a local Member of Parliament, and of the newspapers. Not until 1840 was a petition presented to the House of Commons asking for compensation on account of the great benefits from the invention. Forsyth was short of money and Lord Brougham gave him £400 in 1841. At last, after a wearying wait and heartbreaking appeals, the old man received £200 from the Treasury in 1842. He and his friends were not satisfied and pressed for more. Forsyth wrote to Lord Brougham on 17 February 1843: 'My stipend is not above £160, so what with taxes, etc., I find it difficult to make the two ends meet. Government last year gave me a gratuity of £200. I wish it had been an annuity. It would not have been too much considering what my lock had done in the East and China'.

The parish then had about 1600 people and was about six square miles: he wanted to employ an assistant. An additional award of £1000 was going through the bureaucratic and political systems in the middle of 1843 when Dr Forsyth, one Sunday morning at breakfast when he was cracking open a boiled egg, suddenly died. He never knew that the extra money was coming to him. The £1000 was divided between his niece, grand-nephew, and brother-in-law, for he never married.

CRAFT GUILDS

Trades and their incorporations

Hammermen, fleshers, cordiners and the rest

Craftsmen were socially inferior to merchants but from 1450 onwards began to organise themselves into guilds for mutual support and protection. These bodies had a considerable influence on what was made, and by whom, and of what quality. Glasgow and Edinburgh had fourteen 'incorporated trades' by 1600; Dundee, nine; Perth, eight; Stirling and Aberdeen seven each; and other places one or none.

The crafts in Glasgow had 361 members in 1604. The taylors had 65; the maltsters 55; the cordiners (shoemakers) 50; the weavers, bakers, coopers, skinners, wrights (woodworkers) and hammermen (those who used the hammer in their trade such armourers, blacksmiths, and silversmiths) each had between 20 and 30; the fleshers (butchers) 17; the masons 11; the bonnetmakers 7; the dyers 5; and the surgeons 2.

It was claimed that their aims were of the purest character: to make sure that only qualified people plied their trade in the burgh and that goods of poor quality were not offered there for sale. The truth is different. These guilds spent a lot of effort in keeping away competition and preserving monopolies for their members.

A youth who wanted to enter a craft guild had to serve a very long apprenticeship and probation and pay substantial fees before he could become a full member. The number of apprentices was limited, for example in Glasgow. Entry fees were less for the sons and sons-in-law of men already in the guild. T C Smout says in his *History of the Scottish People* that to many the main benefit of the guild must have been not the opportunity it gave for gain but the defence it gave against the horrors of pauperism: 'Every craft collected regularly for the families of poor distressed members, many ran an almshouse like the trades hospital in Glasgow ... To be a member of a craft guild was to belong to an essentially unadventurous fraternity dedicated to keep both competition and destitution from the door; you could not rise very high as a hammerman or a cordiner, but neither could you fall too low'.

The Incorporations became more and more outmoded during the eighteenth century, but they tried to keep their privileges. Abuses of the system went on until a surprisingly late period. John Begg, watchmaker of Edinburgh, wrote in 1806 that few were better acquainted than he with the monopoly of the Hammermen's

Incorporation of Edinburgh whose charter enabled them to force watchmakers to join them. 'Business', he went on, 'is kept out of the country in consequence of the heavy [entry] dues exacted . . . the trade was driven into the hands of those who were not trained, so that there is scarcely a cloth shop or hardware shop that does not deal in watches, who know no more about a watch than a cow does of a new coined shilling'. His art, he said, should not be shackled by an incorporated body.

The Perth Hammermen refused permission in 1767 for an 'outsider' to work as a watch and clock maker there because three freeman were already in that line of business. The Hammermen told the outsider that if he worked in Perth without permission they would take him to law.

Very high entry fees were demanded in the later eighteenth century by the Edinburgh Hammermen—sometimes as much as £100. Such amounts were impossible to all except the wealthy. But craftsmen could start up businesses in areas such as the New Town of Edinburgh, outside the jurisdiction of the Incorporation.

Parliament abolished the privileges in 1846. Some of the guilds survive to this day, for example in Glasgow, but they are more or less social clubs.

DOMESTIC LIFE

Silver

The treasures and the losses

Silver has a beauty and charm of its own. It is a marvellously adaptable material and the range of objects made of it, both useful and ornamental, is enormous. It is easy to maintain with modern cleaning substances and does not need special care as do other materials such as wood, textiles and leather. Moreover, silver generally has marks or stamps which help in identification and add a great deal to the interest.

Things made in silver or gold have always been in danger from the melting pot. This was especially true at times of disorder such as the Reformation (when church silver vanished) and civil war. Hardly any mediaeval plate made in Scotland has survived.

Other enemies were ignorance and the desire for new-fangled styles. The Kirk Session of Liberton, near Edinburgh, had its communion cups remade in 1763 and recorded that they appeared 'mighty neat and handsome and pleased everybody'. Some kirk sessions are even now not above selling their communion vessels of silver or pewter; as much a tragedy as demolishing fine old buildings.

Silver was being fashioned in Perth in the thirteenth century. The earliest law was passed in 1457 during the reign of James II 'anent the reformation of gold and silver wrocht be Goldsmithes, and to eschew the deceiving done to the kingis lieges'. The craftsman was to take his work to the deacon of his guild and have him examine and mark it. 'And gif faulte be founden therein afterwards, the deakone aforesaid and Goldsmithes gudes sall be in escheit [i.e. forfeit] to the King, and their lives at the kingis will . . . and quhair there is no Goldsmithes bot ane in a towne, he sall shew that warke takened with his awin marke to the head officiates of the towne quhilkis sall have a marke . . . and sall be set to the said warke'.

An Act of 1483 spoke of 'the great damnage and skaithes [harm] that our Sovereign Lordis lieges sustein be the goldsmithes in the minishing [reduction] the fines [fineness] of the silver warke'. This and other laws set up the system of town marks and deacons' marks. The Edinburgh makers had their own Incorporation or guild from the late fifteenth century; the city has always had more silversmiths than any other place.

A royal decree of 1586 and an Act of Parliament of 1587 gave the officials of the goldsmiths' craft in Edinburgh the right to search out gold and silver work and test it for quality. The Edinburgh goldsmiths were given a royal charter in 1687.

The Union of the Crowns in 1603 deprived Edinburgh of the court and in some measure sapped the capital and the nation of great advantages. The Union of the Parliaments in 1707 carried the process further to some extent; but this was compensated for by peace and greater prosperity. The golden age of the Edinburgh silversmiths (if that term can be used) was in the first 50 years or so of the eighteenth century.

Scotland did not take very much to the fripperies of the rococo style nor the artificiality of 'chinoiserie', a craze for the pseudo-Chinese which gripped England from time to time. Instead, sober and elegant lines and craftsmanship were the strong points.

But the country could not forever resist the influence of England. The aristocracy who had connections with England bought silver in London from the end of the seventeenth century; while those who stayed at home and the merchants and trades people bought theirs from Edinburgh, or sometimes local makers. English fashions seeped north to some extent. Then in the 1770s a great change began to be felt. Retailers and silversmiths started to stock items brought from the great centres of manufacture in the south—Birmingham, Sheffield, and London. Moreover, pieces made in England were occasionally bought unmarked and were given Scottish marks.

Objects from the mediaeval era and the fifteenth, sixteenth, and seventeenth centuries are so rare and expensive that they are generally beyond the purse or wallet of the ordinary collector. But the craft of silversmithing revived at the end of the seventeenth century and from that time onwards they are more plentiful.

Scottish Specialities

Thistle cups are rare, early, costly, and beyond the reach of most people. This form has a turned-out lip, an S-shaped handle, and a row of lobes rising up from the foot. Some are as big as a breakfast-cup; others are doll-sized. They seem to have been made from the 1680s to the early 1700s. They were for wine.

Bannock racks, extremely rare, are like very big toast-racks and were to hold the excellent flat, round cakes of oatmeal.

Fish slices, with their large flat blades, gave the craftsman a chance to let his fancy roam and they come in a large variety of designs. They are mostly of the late eighteenth century or the nineteenth.

The country as a whole may have taken to tea later than England did. Pepys first tasted it in 1660 when he wrote in his diary that he 'did send for a cup of tee, (a China drink) of which I never had drank before'. Tea was known in Edinburgh in 1672. A Scot, William Mackintosh of Borlum, recorded in 1729 that 'in lieu of the big quaigh with strong ale and toast and after a dram of good wholesome Scots spirits, there is now the tea-kettle put on the fire, the tea-table, and silver and china equipage brought in with the marmalet, cream and cold tea'.

Tea was expensive in the eighteenth century yet the Scots went in for especially large *teapots*. The early specimens have beautifully functional shapes: spherical

A 'thistle' mug made by James Sympsone of Edinburgh in the late seventeenth century, 3½ inches (9 cm) high. Sympsone was admitted to the Incorporation of Hammermen in 1688; this piece may have been made when he was an apprentice because it has only the maker's mark.

on a moulded foot; or spherical but flattened at the base and top. The lids continue the rounded line; the strainers, although concealed, are prettily made; the handles are elegantly curved; the decoration is slight; the spout, long and straight, shoots out from low in the body—one of the main features.

A celebrated piece of plate is in gold, not silver: little gold plate was made and less survives. It is a teapot made by James Ker of Edinburgh in 1736; one side is engraved with a jockey and horse and 'Legacy 1736'; and the other side with the arms of George II with the Scottish crest. Where the cover and the body join is a band of shells, scrolling foliage, and 'pearls'.

The teapot was a prize in a race run at Leith. Gold teapots were awarded for at least 15 years in this annual event called the King's Plate. Legacy, a black mare, also won the 100 Royal Guineas at Newmarket in the same year.

Urns for coffee and tea were made in a distinctive ovoid form in the 1730s. Their shape has been described as being like a constipated octopus.

Spoons are the most easily collected items and give most chance of acquiring

A typical 'skittle-ball' shaped teapot made by Edward Lothian of Edinburgh in 1733. The assay master was Archibald Ure; the arms are of Gordon of Tobago. English teapots of the time were smaller and did not generally have silver handles.

A stirrup cup made in Edinburgh in 1831. It has the maker's initials, J M. Stirrup cups were for a drink on horseback at the start of the hunt and usually are in the shape of the fox's mask.

the marks of the smaller centres. Basting spoons or hash spoons are hefty and splendid. They sometimes have, screwed into the handle, another useful implement for the kitchen such as a skewer, a marrow scoop, or a spurtle (a rod for stirring porridge). They are $12\frac{1}{2}$ inches (31.7 cm) to 16 inches (40.6 cm) long—much bigger than their English counterparts.

A distinctive shape of spoon is sometimes called the *oar-end*, made from about 1750 to about 1835. It is the fiddle pattern without the shoulders near the bowl. The fiddle pattern gets its name because the handle is shaped like an elongated violin. Some spoons have numbers, and most have the owner's initials, to guard against theft, express ownership or celebrate a marriage. It is an old Scottish custom to put a husband's and wife's initials on things—for example chairs and lintels.

Marrow scoops are long implements with a slender scoop at one end and a wider one at the other. They appeared in the eighteenth century.

Crumb scoops are unique to Scotland: a curved 'blade' on a handle. The 'blade' rests on a table cloth at 90 degrees and is smoothed across the cloth to gather up the crumbs. These implements were in general made from about 1760 to about 1820.

Cowrie shells were mounted in silver as *snuff boxes*. Many were produced in the north-east.

Church Silver

The Church before the Reformation had hundreds of items of gold or silver. Holyrood Abbey had in 1493 several crosses, including one of gold set with thirty precious stones; twelve chalices; candle-sticks; vials; reliquaries; and other things. Aberdeen Cathedral had in 1549 eleven silver chalices and patens.

The Reformers destroyed much. The priests and adherents of the old Church took some. But the bulk was probably melted down or sold to pay for the struggles between Scotland and England.

The new Church gave communion wine to the people as well as to the minister; the cup had thus to be larger. And the chalices of the old Church were not imitated: they were thought papistical. At least some of the cups used in the early years were originally made for ordinary use, not for the communion.

Parliament passed an Act in 1617 decreeing that 'all the paroche Kirkis within this Kingdome be prowydit off Basines and Lavoiris [lavers or jugs] for the ministration of the Sacrament of Baptisme, and of couppes, tablis, and table clothes, for the ministration of the holie Communione'. The penalty for disobeying the Act was the minister's losing a year's stipened.

Communion cups took many forms in the seventeenth century; one special type was made in the north-east. It is beaker-shaped, i.e. like a drinking cup without a stem or foot. Most were made in Aberdeen, some in Edinburgh, and they seem to have been inspired by Continental vessels.

The Marks

Gold and silver are easily debased by the addition of non-precious metals. Doing so is a fraud on the buyer. Spare capital was often invested in objects of gold and silver which could be used or displayed and, when times were hard, melted down or sold. Maintaining proper quality was therefore important in every country. Systems of control were set up—the 'hall marks'.

These marks can usually tell a great deal: the name or at least the initials of the maker, the year, the place, and the standard of the metal (which can vary). Not all the marks, however appear on Scottish silver. The *maker's mark* was usually his initials. But many records have been lost and identification is sometimes impossible in older pieces. The year is often depicted by a letter of the alphabet which was changed annually: the *date letter*. This system applied in Edinburgh from 1681 and in Glasgow from 1819; but only very patchily if at all outside these places and years.

Makers were supposed to get their wares tested by an official of their local craftsmen's guild or by an official of the burgh. A mark was then put on to show that the standard was correct. But methods of testing quality were not exact— much silver is below standard, and some above.

Itinerant craftsmen made many spoons and other small articles such as brooches and used their own variations of a town mark. The rules were tidied up in 1836: an Act of Parliament laid down that all work done in Scotland had to be assayed and marked in Edinburgh or Glasgow. But some makers continued to mark pieces themselves.

Aberdeen: The mark is usually the town's name abbreviated—ABD is the most usual but AB and ABDN are found. Another mark, at the beginning of the eighteenth century, was three castles from the town's coat of arms. This became debased to three crosses.

Arbroath: A portcullis, from the town's arms.

Canongate: The early mark, about 1550, was a stag 'couchant' with a cross between the antlers; from about 1690 a stag's head 'erased' (jagged at the neck as if it had been torn from the body) with a cross between the antlers; and much later, in a debased form, the head without the cross. The burgh really comprised part of the Royal Mile in Edinburgh; the two burghs were combined in 1853.

Dundee: A pot of lilies, from the town's coat of arms, or very rarely the word DUNDEE. The town was devastated by Cromwell's forces and seems to have taken a long time to recover.

Edinburgh: A castle with three towers. Date letters have been used since 1681 and the maker's mark, from 1457. Standard marks were the initials of the Deacon of the craft from 1457 to 1681; the initials of the assay master from 1681 to 1759; a thistle from 1759; a lion rampant from 1975. Only Edinburgh used the Deacon's mark.

Elgin: The letters ELN or ELGIN; or the figure of a mother and child; or the figure of St Egidius (St Giles); or a portrayal of the west front of the cathedral.

Glasgow: The city's coat of arms—a tree, bell, bird, and fish with a ring in its mouth. The details are sometimes hard to see. Date letters also started to be used, in 1681. They were given up in the early eighteenth century, were revived again in 1819, and continued until the assay office in the city was closed in 1964 for lack of business. Other marks are, a maker's mark: the letters S, O, and E whose meaning is obscure: the standard mark of a lion rampant, from 1819.

Greenock: The history of this town as a centre for the craft is curious indeed. It was until recently thought to have been very active. A leading authority wrote: 'Quite

Silver marks. Left to right: Edinburgh, Thistle, Glasgow, Lion Rampant.

a remarkable number of important pieces of Greenock silver have survived.' The remarkable thing about many Greenock pieces is that in fact they were made in Calcutta. The confusion arose because their marks—an anchor, a thistle, and the makers initials JH—were wrongly ascribed. The Calcutta firm of John Hunt, later John Hunt and Company, is first mentioned in records in 1788 and last mentioned in 1816. The British in India commissioned a lot of silver for their homes and messes, and as prizes for sporting events.

It is possible that the marks of Scottish, Indian, Canadian, South African, West Indian, and other craftsmen are still mixed up. Greenock was, however, reasonably active from about 1780 to about 1830.

Inverness: The letters INS. Also found is a dromedary, which is one of the supporters of the town's coat of arms.

Montrose: A punning rose: mostly on spoons of the early nineteenth century.

Perth: A lamb with a St Andrew's flag until the early eighteenth century; a double-headed eagle (from the town's arms) until about 1830; then a single-headed eagle. Few silversmiths worked in Perth.

Peterhead: The mark is PHD.

St Andrews: Very rare; a St Andrew's cross.

Tain: The mark is the name of the town in full; or the figure of St Dithaces between the letters SD. His shrine at Tain before the Reformation was perhaps the most important in the country. The Kings went there every year on pilgrimage and gave great gifts.

Wick: The mark is the name of the town in full; most of the pieces made there are of later years.

The Government could not resist raising taxes from the trade. A special mark of the sovereign's head in profile was stamped on the articles to show that duty had been paid. This was put on in Edinburgh from 1784 and in Glasgow from 1819; the duty and the mark were abolished in 1890. The law meant that all silver made in Scotland had to be sent to Edinburgh or, later, Glasgow, to be marked and taxed.

Notable royal occasions have been commemorated by special marks. They are the Silver Jubilee of George V and Queen Mary (their double profiles, on silver made from 1933 to 1935), the coronation of Queen Elizabeth (profile, 1952 and 1953) and the Jubilee of Queen Elizabeth (also profile, 1977).

Deceptions
Marks have from time to time been forged—a grave offence—but the risk to the collector is slight. A forgery may be to make the date appear different; or to pretend that the craftsman was someone else; or to change the place of

Top:
Edinburgh marks from a communion cup made in about 1645. They are of the maker, Patrick Borthwick; the town mark; and the deacon, Adam Lamb.

Above:
A rare cup and cover, 8¼ inches (21 cm) high, made in Edinburgh in 1708 by James Sympsone. The assay master was Edward Penman. It is solid and satisfying. The lid when turned over forms a dish.

manufacture. This can be done in several ways. Genuine marks have been cut out of an original object and incorporated in a new. Casts and moulds have been made of small items, especially spoons; but cast silver is rigid and lacks the springiness of the genuine article. A doubtful piece can be referred to the antique plate committee of the Goldsmith's Company in London for adjudication.

Some silversmiths in the smaller places put on their goods imitation Edinburgh marks. The aim was to dodge the duty but at the same time to give their customers a guarantee that the work was of the proper standard. One of the people who did this was Andrew Black of Alloa who was working from about 1830 to about 1870.

George Heriot

Little is known about the lives of the silversmiths but one distinguished himself and founded his own memorial: George Heriot (1563–1624), who set up Heriot's Hospital in Edinburgh. This is a school in a beautiful seventeenth-century building.

Heriot's career began in a shop or 'booth' in Edinburgh, only seven feet square. But James VI made him jeweller to his consort, Anne of Denmark, in 1597 and jeweller to the King himself in 1601. Heriot was not only jeweller to the King and Queen but also their banker, moneylender, and pawnbroker. These were common sidelines for some Edinburgh goldsmiths until modern banking was invented. The Queen seems to have had dealings amounting to £50,000 sterling in the 10 years before James came to the throne of England.

James went to England in the spring of 1603 and Heriot soon followed him: one of many Scots who did so to the mortification of the English courtiers and others. No doubt Heriot was anxious to make sure of his royal debts as well as to get more business.

He had so many orders in 1609 that he could not get hold of enough workmen; and at the same period the Queen owed him about £18,000 for jewels and other things. Heriot had some difficulty in getting the money. Most of his wealth was assigned, shortly before his death, to Edinburgh Town Council for the education of the children of decayed burgesses and freemen 'for the honour and due regard which I bear to . . . Edinburgh'. The sum was £23,625. Sir Walter Scott's novel *The Fortunes of Nigel* depicts Heriot—but Scott's account of him is fictional.

Pewter
The tappit hen, chopin, mutchkin and others

Pewter was once so commonplace that people hardly gave it a thought. Now it turns up in nearly every antique shop, the finest specimens fetch large sums, and there has been faking. Most Scottish pewter has emigrated.

Old Scottish pewter is generally of better than average quality in the workmanship and the metal. But it is comparatively scarce. Dented, worn, or leaky pieces were valuable as scrap and were melted down to make new; and the country did not have plentiful supplies of tin, one of the main ingredients of pewter. (The other is lead; the lower the proportion of lead, the better the pewter.)

Tappit hen of the eighteenth century, 12 inches (30.3 cm) high. It is called the 'crested' type because of the knob on top of the lid. Sold by Sotheby's in 1974 for £399.

The most famous and highly prized Scottish items are tappit hens: vessels of elegant and satisfying design. Nobody is sure about the origin of the curious name. It may be from a fanciful resemblance of the vessels to a crested hen because some of them have a knob on the lid, but that theory may be far-fetched. The shape may have been copied from French flagons but again the origin is doubtful and does not really matter.

Most tappit hens hold one Scottish pint, which was the equivalent of three Imperial pints. The earliest known to have survived dates from about 1669 but most are from between about 1750 and 1850.

Other measures were made in the same delightful shape: the chopin ($1\frac{1}{2}$ Imperial pints) and the mutchkin ($\frac{3}{4}$ Imperial pint). But Scottish measures were chaotic for centuries: they tended to vary from place to place. The British Government tried to impose the English standards and did not succeed until a firm Act of Parliament was passed in 1855. All this means that tappit hens are found in, it is said, 19 different sizes. Many specimens have a blob of metal inside the neck and about two inches (5 cm) from the rim. It showed how far up the vessel ought to be filled. This feature is called the plook (or plowk or plouk, i.e. pimple).

Another measure used in pubs was in a patriotic thistle shape. The outline is like a tumbler with a bulbous lower half. A publican using this type of measure could not empty out the drink completely unless the bottom was tipped up very high. What was not poured out slipped back and became profit for the publican. Perhaps the shape was badly designed or perhaps the aim was to cheat. Thistle measures were prohibited by law in 1907, many were destroyed or given to the rag-and-bone man, and the survivors are rare.

A distinctive object is the pot-bellied measure, which is roughly pear-shaped These measures vary in height from about 4 inches (10 cm) to 11 inches (27.5 cm). Most date from the seventeenth century and they were seldom used after the middle of the eighteenth. They are rare and some of them have lids which have been added at a later date.

Plates which are Scottish may be unrecognised and may be masquerading as English because they lack the marks that should distinguish them. It is likely that plates tended to be comparatively deep because of the national taste for foods such as broth and porridge.

Hard-up congregations bought pewter communion cups, wine flagons, bread plates and offering plates. The name of the church was sometimes engraved on them. Church pewter has survived in greater quantity than household pewter because it was carefully kept and little used.

Pewter tarnishes with time and with exposure to air and becomes scaly. Its surface may become blemished with pock marks and small bubbling eruptions which can never be cured. Collectors are always arguing about how much cleaning ought to be done. Too little means an unsightly object. Too much makes the object look garish and new, destroys half the charm, and can harm initials and marks. Cleaning is done with furniture polish, metal polish, caustic soda, acid, emery paper, or buffing wheels. But it is better to do the minimum cleaning.

Faking has been going on for at least 50 years. Pewter objects are made from moulds. It is not difficult to make a mould from a genuine piece and cast a reproduction from that. Signs of age can be added artificially and older fakes have, through the years, acquired real signs of age. Genuine but damaged pieces have been heavily restored. Experience or a reliable dealer are the best guides.

Marks

Newly-made and highly polished pewter looks like silver, especially at a distance and in indoor light. That was one reason why people bought it. Sometimes the makers helped along the deception by putting on their products marks which look like the hallmarks on silver. The Goldsmiths' Company in London complained about this practice from time to time with success.

The marks, if a piece does have any, are:

Four small *imitation hall marks*. Examples are a thistle, a rose, the maker's initials, and the name of the town where he worked, in abbreviated form. They

One of the two Edinburgh 'touch plates' for pewterers' marks. The other plate has only two.

were adopted in the eighteenth century.

Quality marks. In the sixteenth century, a hammer with a crown. In the seventeenth century and later, a thistle. In the first half of the eighteenth century, a crowned letter X (this was imitated from the English makers but the English tended to use it indiscriminately).

The maker's private mark or 'touch'. Pewterers who were members of the Hammermen in Edinburgh used at first a mark of a castle, the date, and the maker's initials. But this was given up after the middle of the eighteenth century; and the marks after that are rather like the London ones. Examples are a rose and the maker's name, or a device such as 'a bird with outstretched wings looking over its left shoulder and standing upon a globe'.

Capacity marks. Care had to be taken against short measure in taverns and, until 1826, the Dean of Guild tested measures—if they were correct he applied a stamp. This usually has the town's arms, or part of the arms, and the Dean of

Guild's initials. From 1826 to 1835, the town's arms, or part of the arms, with the initials of the King on either side and a crown above. The form does, however, vary. From 1835 to 1878, much the same as for 1826–1835 but often with the date of the test below. From 1878, a crown, the initials of the sovereign, and a number which signifies the district of the Inspectorate of Weights and Measures.

One touch is square, with a ship in full sail, and slogans such as 'Success to the British Colonies. Maxwell,' and 'Success to the United States of America. Maxwell.' The word London also appears; but Stephen Maxwell (about 1784–1820) worked in Glasgow. The 'London' may have been to encourage sales.

Several guilds of pewterers in Britain kept special plates on which members struck their marks. This was to keep proper records of who was properly qualified and enrolled in the craft. Only plates of Edinburgh and London have survived. The Edinburgh ones have a curious history. They were presented in 1871 to the National Museum of Antiquities of Scotland in a small wooden chest bound with iron. Nobody quite knew what they really were and a bizarre theory was put forward. This said that they had belonged to the descendants of Johnny Faa, a famous gipsy. James V gave him the title of Lord and Count of Little Egypt and Johnny Faa punished members of his tribe who broke the law. The theory was that the plates were given to that tribe as a kind of licence for its members to work at the crafts of the hammermen; and that the plates would be brought yearly to Edinburgh to be stamped. Their real purpose was as registers for the marks of pewterers in the Edinburgh Hammermen. Perhaps they were also specimens of the standard of pewter to be used. These two plates give a record of the marks from about 1590 to 1764. One is covered in marks but the other has only two.

The loss of the craft

Pewter declined because better materials were devised. Iron with a coating of tin, called white iron, was a strong competitor from about 1725. A better imitation of silver was invented in the 1740s—Sheffield plate, which is copper between two thin sheets of silver. Britannia metal, an alloy of tin and antimony, was a competitor from about 1820—it was easier to work and to ornament with fanciful flourishes.

Tea ousted beer as the people's everyday drink from the beginning of the nineteenth century onwards; and tea does not taste right in pewter. Pottery and porcelain became comparatively cheap in the second half of the eighteenth century and hit the pewterers' trade. The great potter Josiah Wedgwood (1730–1795), whose factory in Staffordshire was in its heyday the biggest in Europe, recorded in his diary on 5 June 1775, when he was in Cornwall: 'I was glad . . . to hear that the price of tin was got up from 50 to 60 sh per cwt. for I had been seriously advised by some of my friends before I left London not to trust myself among the miners of Cornwall, the tin trade then being low, and they, being persuaded that the use of Queen's ware [an attractive and popular kind of earthenware invented by Wedgwood] was the cause of it, had already shown some instances of their displeasure at that manufacture. However, we found them all very civil'.

Jewellery

Love and the evil eye

Jewellery with Scottish themes was fashionable in Victorian times, from the 1840s and especially in the 1860s. Brooches set with cairngorms, grouse claws mounted in silver as brooches, miniature dirks, shields, and claymores ornamented with 'Scotch pebbles' or agates, Luckenbooth brooches, thistles, and St Andrew's crosses, are typical of the period.

A women's magazine reported in 1867: 'Scotch jewellery as well as Scotch costume is *de rigeur*, and the badges of the different clans are worn as brooches, earrings, buckles, and as the centre of shoe rosettes'. Another magazine said in 1878: 'The effect of the . . . rich colours of the clan-tartan is enhanced by a multitude of engraved silver buttons, shoulder brooches, embossed buckles, jewelled dirks etc. Until, in a full and archaeologically correct Highland costume—there is a perfectly dazzling combination of silver—burnished, dead, and frosted—combined with precious stones'.

Skill was needed in making some of the jewellery and a flourishing industry grew in Edinburgh, Birmingham, and Germany. The Scottish craftsmen were highly praised for the products they sent to great international exhibitions of the arts. France took a fancy to Scottish themes.

The use of 'Scotch pebbles' or agates in jewellery was old when the Victorians took an interest. An advertisement in the *Caledonian Mercury* in 1749 said: 'TO THE CURIOUS—John Fairweather, Lapidary, at Clockmill, in the corner of St Ann's Yards Edinburgh, cuts all kinds of Scots Pebbles after the best manner into all shapes at the lowest prices, and has, with his new invented machinery, lately made several pebble watch cases to the satisfaction of the most curious, and at so low a price as one guinea and a half the piece. He being the only Scotsman hitherto that has made any, notwithstanding there are other pretenders'. Lapidary work flourished in Edinburgh from the late eighteenth century.

The heart, or Luckenbooth brooch, made from about 1700, is still popular as a souvenir. The name comes from the luckenbooths or locked booths around the High Kirk of St Giles (St Giles' Cathedral), Edinburgh, where the silversmiths carried on business. But these brooches were made all over the country. They are shaped like a heart or two hearts intertwined and sometimes they have a crown on the upper part. They were given when a couple became engaged and they were also for magical purposes. The story went that nursing mothers wore them to stop witches stealing their milk, or harming their babies; and they were also to ward off the evil eye.

The type in the shape of two intertwined hearts is rather like the letter M; this, combined with the crown, inspired a story that they were linked with Mary Queen of Scots. The story is untrue, although heart-shaped jewellery was popular in her time among rich people in Scotland, England and Continental countries. The heart shape later came down in society. It also travelled; heart-shaped brooches were made in Canada in the nineteenth century. These examples are identical with the Scottish but are flimsier.

A writer at the end of the eighteenth century said of the Luckenbooth brooch: 'They always fix it to girls somewhere on the left hip and on boys about the middle of the left thigh.' The same author said he once met an old woman who had worn a brooch fixed on her clothes upon the left hip for more than 50 years 'to preserve her from mischief '.

Some brooches were given when a couple became engaged; their initials and the date are sometimes inscribed on the back, perhaps with words such as 'Where this I give I wish to live.'

The biggest Luckenbooth brooches are about two inches and the smallest are so minute that they are difficult to handle. Most are of silver and a very few of gold. Early examples, of the eighteenth century, are simple and later ones have agates, semi-precious stones, or glass disguised as jewels.

Brooches for fastening the plaid were made in the seventeenth and eighteenth centuries. They are round and the biggest are as much as eight inches (20 cm) across. They are of brass or silver but the bigger ones are generally of brass—probably because silver was too costly. The finest, which are also the earliest, are divided up into compartments or panels and have engraved flowers, interlaced bands, and animals such as wild cats and griffons. The poorest have scanty zig-zag lines or no decoration at all.

Women wore these brooches and men fastened their plaids with pins. (It used to be thought that the silver ones were for women and the brass for men.)

Pebble jewellery: necklace, earrings and buckles of polished agates set in gold-coloured metal and enamel. The set was given in the 1780s to the National Museum of Antiquities of Scotland.

Below:
Brooch of gold set with artificial pearls and imitation jewels and made in about 1825. It is $1\frac{3}{4}$ inches (4.4 cm) across.

Right:
Brooch of silver with engraving and set with polished pebbles and citrines. It was made in about 1850 and is $2\frac{3}{4}$ inches (6.9 cm) across.
The design was suggested by an eighth-century brooch called the Hunterston Brooch after the place in Ayrshire where it was found.

Silver brooches seem to have been made from about 1700 and were gifts from a man to his fiancée: they have two pairs of initials and a date. Their decoration is of thistles or criss-crossed lines cut into the metal or in niello (niello is a black alloy of silver). Brooches of silver with niello decoration have been called Glasgow brooches for no good reason. It is thought that some were made by tinkers or in Gaelic *ceardan* (the singular of the word is *ceard*, pronounced 'caird'). Tinkers may have done a lot of work in metal and stone. But most eighteenth-century brooches were made by silversmiths.

Plaid brooches must have been plentiful but are now scarce. Making of the authentic article died out towards the end of the eighteenth century but the silversmiths of Glasgow, Inverness, and elsewhere took up the making of brooches for more sophisticated customers. The products were quite different. The kind with a circular rim of metal and a cairngorm in the middle is a 'marriage' of a mediaeval type and the plaid type. Large specimens are to be seen on the left shoulders of pipers and smaller ones on women's clothes.

The country was fortunate in having raw materials. Cairngorms are a brown form of quartz. Agates are plentiful. Amethysts, topazes, aquamarines, and other semi-precious stones are found. A woman who lived near Braemar in the second half of the eighteenth century, called the 'Old Woman of Stones', once dreamed that a huge cairngorm beckoned to her from the rocks of Beinn a'Bhuird—and she found there a crystal weighing 52 pounds (23.5 kg) which can be seen at Braemar Castle. John Grant of Ryvoan found a stone weighing 50 pounds on Ben Macdhui; he presented it to Queen Victoria who gave him £50 in return. But not all the cairngorms used in Scottish jewellery came from Scotland and some 'cairngorms' are really coloured glass. A true quartz cannot, however, be scratched by steel.

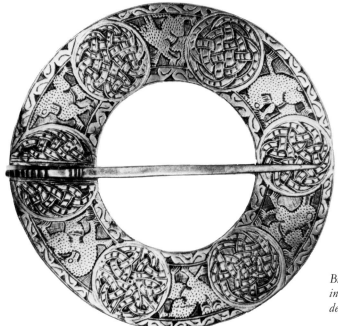

Brass brooch of the seventeenth century, almost 7 inches (17.8 cm) across, ornamented with interlaced designs and fabulous beasts.

Silver brooch with the maker's mark WM, possibly William Mackay and possibly made in Edinburgh in 1840. It is about 2½ inches (5.7 cm) wide.

Polished granite—red and greyish-black—was mounted as brooches in Aberdeen from about 1875 onwards.

Pearls come from a species of mussel which lives in rivers. They are not as beautiful or valuable as the oriental sort but the Crown of Scotland is adorned with them. A dealer in Edinburgh, Moritz Unger, announced in 1863 that he would take unlimited quantities of freshwater pearls at fixed prices.

The *Illustrated London News* reported on 17 September 1864:

In some rural districts, the peasantry are making their fortunes by pearl-seeking for only a few hours a day . . . Mr. Unger even provides his pearl-gatherers with a waterproof dress, so that their labour may be as little detrimental to their health as possible.

It was in the summer of 1863 that the fever of pearl searching broke out thoroughly. Mr. Unger made his appearance, and bought up all that he could at prices which perfectly startled the people; and, as a consequence, young and old, male and female, rushed like ducks to the water, and waded, dived, and swam till the excitement became so intense as to be called by many the 'pearl fever' . . . The smell of heaps upon heaps of putrid mussels tells the magnitude of the slaughter.

The report says that many of the pearls were disposed of at £1 each, others at 25s (£1.25) and one or two at £2, while a great number ranged from 7s 6d (37.5p) to 15s (75p) each. 'But by far the greater proportion were either entirely useless, or on account of their smallness, bad shape, or colour were parted with for a mere trifle . . . The general cry was that so much exposure of the body was likely to introduce a variety of diseases such as had not hitherto been known in the place; but no such effects made their appearance.' Mounds of opened mussels rotted on the banks.

After this bonanza, demand fell away somewhat but still stayed steady. Victoria herself had a fine collection of the pearls, and today a few are still being fished for.

Porcelain and Pottery

From Delftware to 'wally dugs'

Porcelain and pottery are very different. Porcelain is fired at a higher temperature; is translucent; reverberates, when struck, like a bell; can be shaped into delicate and even elaborate forms. Pottery is easier to make; is opaque; less adaptable; less suitable for exotic coloured decoration. Porcelain needs special ingredients; pottery needs clay which can be found in suitable form in many places.

The special ingredients of true porcelain are china clay and china stone; both are decayed forms of granite. The art of making porcelain was unknown to Europe until the early eighteenth century; until then it was a secret and a monopoly of the Chinese and Japanese.

Its qualities, comparative rarity, and high cost made it highly desirable. The secret of its manufacture was discovered at Meissen, near Dresden, by an alchemist, Johann Friedrich Bottger, and a physicist and mathematician, Ehrenfried Walter von Tschirnhaus.

This knowledge was extremely valuable and soon leaked out of the factory at Meissen, helped on its way by bribery and other skulduggery. Britain started to make porcelain in the mid-eighteenth century but it was in general not the true or 'hard paste' kind but another called 'artificial' or 'soft paste'. Its ingredients are white clay and a meltable substance such as ground glass. Cornwall was and is a great source of china clay and china stone. Bone china is another substance, made of fine clay and animals' burned bones; it was invented in Britain in the mid-eighteenth century. Scotland has plenty of clay but no china stone or china clay.

Delftware

A kind of treasure has been found buried by the bank of the Clyde at the end of James Watt Street, Glasgow. The area was the site of a factory that made Delftware between 1749 and 1810. But identifying what was made there has been difficult because the products were not given a distinctive mark. Excavations on the site have revealed fragments of pottery. There is little doubt that these fragments are rubbish from the factory and that they will help to show what the products were.

Delftware is pottery glazed with oxide (ashes) of tin and was made in several European countries; but they practically all depended upon Cornwall for their supplies of tin. The name delft comes from the town in the Netherlands but is a misnomer because the ware was made in other places before it was ever made in Delft.

The glaze is basically white and opaque but can be decorated with colours— blues, greens, yellow, purples and reds. This makes it far more attractive in appearance than the brown and green pottery, glazed with lead, which it partially replaced especially in the eighteenth century.

Delftware, however, tended to chip and was not good at resisting heat. It was replaced by longer-lasting pottery in the second half of the eighteenth century.

Plate made by the Verreville factory, Glasgow, between about 1825 and 1830 and showing the Park Theatre, New York. The Glasgow factories did a lot of trade with North America.

Glasgow may have been the last place in Britain to turn out delftware. The factory, called the Delftfield pottery, was founded by Robert and Laurence Dinwiddie, who were also merchants, Robert Findlay, and Patrick Nisbet. Robert Dinwiddie (1692–1770) was later Lieutenant-Governor of Virginia; his brother Laurence (1696–1764) was Lord Provost of Glasgow in 1742 and 1743, supported the Government during the '45, and became a founder of the Glasgow Arms Bank in 1750. Findlay was a leading citizen and a partner in a tannery. Nisbet is a shadowy figure.

The capital was about £12,000, the factory was on 8 acres (about 3.2 hectares), and the buildings were large and solid. One of them was described as 'mair liker a kirk'. A potter was brought from London, named John Bird. The clay tried was found unsuitable and other supplies had to be brought from Northern Ireland; and the first firing was a disaster because the clay supports which held the pots in the kiln collapsed. But success came, and an advertisement in the *Edinburgh Evening Courant* of 23 January 1752 said: 'The Proprietors of the DELFT MANUFACTORY at GLASGOW having, with a great deal of Trouble and Charge, established this Branch of Business, of making all Sorts and Kinds of Delft or Lime Ware . . . and as their Ware is brought to a great Degree of Perfection, and gives Satisfaction both at home and abroad, and as it is sold at as low a price as English Delft Ware, it is expected that all Lovers of their Country will encourage this manufactory'.

Not only Scots supported the factory, for in 1771 no fewer than 2600 pieces of delftware were sent to Philadelphia and 12,828 to Virginia, and 19,000 pieces of delft and stoneware to Maryland.

The factory had started in 1766 to make stoneware, which is dense and heavy and fired at a high temperature, and in 1770 to make creamware, which is light and strong and can be worked into delicate shapes. But in 1810 the factory was closed, the buildings and land sold, the workshops destroyed, and the moulds and patterns taken over by another pottery.

Among the pieces thought to be from the Delftfield pottery are a bowl inscribed 'Joy & Success to Robert Gilchrist Lord Sheriff of Hamilton 1761' and another bowl with 'Success to the town of Glasgow'. These and others have sprays of flowers and whip-like tendrils. The tendrils may be a 'trade mark' of the factory. Excavations at the site will, with a bit of luck, clear up a lot of questions, as has happened at several sites of potteries in England and elsewhere.

Verreville

The Finnieston district of Glasgow is now dreary indeed; but was in the early nineteenth century a village of thatched cottages set in green fields with fine trees and a pleasing view of the Clyde; merchants and their families came from Glasgow for their holidays. The only complaints were about illicit removal of the fine sandy soil and about coaches and horses being raced through the village.

Finnieston was dominated by a brick cone 120 feet high which was built in the 1770s for making glass ware: the factory was called Verreville (glass town).

Earthenware was also made there from early years in the factory's history and porcelain from 1820. Large numbers of workmen had to be brought in at the beginning from the Low Countries and England but they were not always satisfactory and Scottish workers were trained in the crafts. A potter who had bolted from the Wedgwood factory in Staffordshire wrote to his former employer from Verreville in 1826:

Sir,

From a sincere sense, and repentance of my former sins, and transactions, especially against you, I humbly ask you pardon, and hope you will forgive the same, and if you will take me in your employ again, I will work six days, and four half nights for 15s per week for three years (if the Lord spare me) in order to pay you the principal, and interest, what I owe you.

In hope of your accepting this offer

I remain, Sir, your most obedient servant, JOHN MAYER

P.S. Honoured Sir, I hope you will give order to Mr H. Greatbach (works manager) to send for me and I solemnly assure you by the God of Jacob you shall never have occasion to repent it. I only wish for an opportunity to convince you of my amendment in life, and practice.

Ownership of Verreville changed from time to time. R A Kidston took over in 1838, brought skilled workers from other factories, and in a short time was making objects of high quality in both 'body' and glaze. Excavations at the site have recently recovered about half a ton (508 kg) of broken pottery from this period. This has helped to identify many of the products made there. Profit did not, however, follow art, and another owner, Robert Cochrane, took over in 1847. He went in for less fancy and costly ware, and did a great line in two-pound jam jars; the firm finally closed in 1918.

Mark of the Verreville factory, Glasgow.

Bell's Pottery

A large factory in Glasgow, called Bell's Pottery, produced typically Victorian wares of many kinds. They are usually marked J & MP Bell, with the name of the pattern. The works was also called the Glasgow Pottery. The site was in the Port Dundas district on the banks of the Forth and Clyde canal, an asset for the transport of clay and coal.

One of the specialities was Parian ware, a white pottery with a finish like marble. It was made by many factories in Britain; and especially for figures and busts imitating sculpture. The name is from Parian marble, an exceptionally fine type.

Blue and white earthenware was the major line and was done in dozens of designs such as the 'willow pattern' and 'triumphal car'. The triumphal car is a chariot drawn by two leopards; in the background are temples, palms, and palaces. The firm did a brisk trade with the Far East. A huge amount of Bell's output went to the American market—indeed this was the case with most of the Glasgow factories from Delftfield on.

The two partners were John and Matthew Bell, who built a fine mansion on the banks of the river Kelvin in Glasgow. The building later became Queen Margaret College, for women students at Glasgow University, and is now part of the BBC's Scottish headquarters. John Bell collected Old Masters and some people in the city believed that they were duds. Pencil jottings on his will were thought to bequeath the house and the collection to the city but the house and paintings were auctioned in 1881. Many of the paintings were sold at Christie's and against all expectations and to the chagrin of Glasgow went for large sums. The Bells were shrewd and John had taken good advice when he was building up the collection.

Other pottery

Innumerable potteries scattered around the country, especially in the Lowlands, produced simple wares for ordinary homes. Hawkers were the middlemen. An account written in 1793 said: 'They come under the description of itinerant merchants and tinkers, who, in the summer season, with their horses and asses loaded with kitchen utensils of every description for the husbandman and labourer, as well as the mechanic, perambulate the country. For these wares they receive in part payment old clothes and rags, which are now carefully kept by the cottager's wife for the purpose of upholding herself and cupboard in the articles necessary for the shelves, and now the tea table. In this instance we find vanity acting an useful part, in furnishing the papermakers with the raw material for that useful art.' Paper was then made from rags. The china wholesalers also accepted scrap metal of all kinds, skins, and anything else which had some value.

Among the humble objects made in pottery were jam jars, drainage pipes, and, during the nineteenth century, sanitary ware. Clay tobacco pipes were vital. Many were made in and around Glasgow, but Thomas Carlyle wrote in 1840 to a friend in Edinburgh and enclosing half a sovereign:

I am in pressing want of Tobacco-Pipes; this small gold coin is to procure me through your kindness, Tobacco-Pipes from Edinburgh. Down in the Canongate not far from

Victorian ornament for mantelpiece, by J and M P Bell of Glasgow.

John Knox's House there used to dwell, and labour that eminent Pipe-maker Thomas White. He, probably is no longer alive; but his representatives, his manufactory, must still be there, and pipes of the same eminent fabric. The kind of pipes I was wont to get there were his best, and biggest; 3s 6d a gross . . . There is nothing more to be added except the propriety of straitly charging the people to be most careful in the packing, and then to ship them by first steamer for my hurry is considerable.

Victorian figures

Nothing seems to need ornamentation more than the British mantelpiece, and for generations the potters have supplied this need. Victorian pottery figures of famous people and appealing animals, called Staffordshire figures, were a folk art and are now very desirable.

They are called Staffordshire but were made in other places as well—for example at Pollokshaws, then a village near Glasgow, and at Portobello and Prestonpans, both near Edinburgh. These figures are crudely modelled because they were made from only two or three moulds, were mass-produced, and sold for only a few pence or a few shillings. They do, however, reflect what interested ordinary and even more sophisticated people at the time; their heyday was roughly from about the 1840s to the 1880s. Only very rarely were they given a maker's mark, which is a pity for collectors. Ones with Scottish subjects may not have been made in Scotland at all.

The biggest group of portraits is naturally of *royalty*: Victoria, Albert, and their children—especially the elder children of their large family. After a while public interest seems to have waned in the latest prince or princess.

Politicians are of the kind that appealed to the mass of the people: Gladstone the Liberal; Peel who let cheap corn into the country; Kossuth the Hungarian patriot who led a rebellion against the Austro-Hungarian Empire; and Garibaldi who unified the Italian nation. Garibaldi is often shown with his British friend Colonel Peard, which shows British insularity. Disraeli the Conservative is rare and usually goes in a pair with Gladstone.

Personalities of the *theatre* may have appealed to the better-off end of the market: Garrick, Kemble, Macready, and Jenny Lind.

Military heroes came to the fore during the Crimean War and the Indian Mutiny—for example, Lord Raglan, commander of the army, and General Sir George Cathcart who was leading a charge when he was shot through the heart. Florence Nightingale had her honoured place.

Crime was always of absorbing interest, and the more lurid the better. Frederick George Manning and his Swiss wife Marie murdered the wife's lover and buried him under the kitchen floor of their house in Bermondsey, London; they were hanged on the roof of a London prison in 1849 in the presence of a huge crowd.

Animals included spaniels, poodles, greyhounds, zebras, tigers, and horses. Dylan Thomas wrote in *Under Milk Wood* of 'curtained fernpot, text, and trinket harmonium . . . china dog and rosy tin tea caddy'. China dogs were called 'wally dugs' in Scotland (wally means china, as in *wally* teeth).

Highland Jessie became a folk heroine for the Victorians and one of the first people from ordinary ranks of life to be shown in a Staffordshire figure. Her fame is from an incident during the Indian Mutiny. About 350 European men, 350 women and children, and 120 sick and 300 loyal sepoys and other Indians took refuge on 17 May 1857 in the Residency at Lucknow, capital of Oudh; the building was only a private house with a few defences hastily thrown up. They were besieged by about 10,000 disciplined troops and some irregulars. The people in the Residency suffered appallingly. A relieving force under Major General Sir Henry Havelock arrived on 16 September, but all that it could do was to reinforce the garrison, not defeat the besieging forces. Seven more weeks of suffering had to be endured. The survivors were in extremes of despair in the second week of November when Highland Jessie, wife of a Corporal Brown, shrieked that she could hear the pipes. An army under Sir Colin Campbell was approaching Lucknow. Among his troops were his favourite regiment, the 93rd Highlanders, and the tune that Highland Jessie heard was 'The Campbells are Coming'. Highland Jessie was depicted with rifle in hand and supporting a wounded soldier; or with a soldier sitting beside her.

Sir Henry Havelock, who died of cholera soon after the relief of Lucknow and was a hero of the war, was commemorated by the potters. So too was Sir Colin Campbell (1792–1863), who is shown with a Scottish bonnet or wearing trews. Campbell was the son of John Macliver, a carpenter in Glasgow; but he was befriended as a child and youth by his uncle, a Campbell and officer in the army. The young man was introduced to the Duke of York, commander-in-chief of the army, as a candidate for a commission. The Duke cried out: 'What, another of the Clan!' and a note was made of his name as Campbell. He fought with distinction in the Peninsular War, China, and the Crimea, saved the British Empire in India, and died a field marshal and a baron—Lord Clyde. The figures of him may have been done after his Indian campaigns or after his feats in the Crimean War—he directed the 93rd Highlanders when they repulsed the Russians at Balaclava and he was outstanding at other battles.

James Braidwood (1800–1861), superintendent of the London Fire Brigade, was a notable pioneer and a public benefactor, and died sensationally—all things that made him suitable for commemoration. He was born in Edinburgh, educated at the High School, joined the police, and became head of the fire brigade in 1824. He started to improve its efficiency. A dreadful fire in the same year destroyed part of the High Street including the steeple of the historic Tron Church. An ironmonger's shop also caught fire—and it contained gunpowder. Braidwood went in and at great risk took out first one and then another barrel of powder. He published in 1830 a pamphlet on improving ways of fire fighting and became in 1832 head of the London Fire-engine Establishment, then supported by the different insurance companies; he showed marvellous energy and perseverance. Braidwood was on duty at a huge outbreak on 22 June 1861 at a wharf and warehouse in Tooley Street, London Bridge, when he was crushed by a falling wall and buried in the ruins. His body, horribly mutilated, was recovered two days later. He was so famous throughout London and the manner of his death was so extraordinary that the whole of the capital came to a halt during his funeral.

The bells of all the City churches were tolled and all the shops were shut. Braidwood's figure is shown in his fireman's uniform of helmet and epauletted coat, with his right hand on a pedestal. The figure is labelled BRAIDWOOD.

Wemyss ware, made in or near Kirkcaldy, Fife, has been showing signs of a revival of interest among collectors. Similar items of pottery were made by several factories including Methven and Sons of Kirkcaldy and the Fife Pottery, Gallatown: one of the characteristics is lavish floral decoration on toilet sets, mugs, jars for biscuits and preserves, vases of all sorts, umbrella stands, and garden seats. Animals and commemorative ware were made too.

'Art' potteries of note were the Allander pottery in Milngavie, near Glasgow, run by Hugh Allan from about 1902 to 1908; and the Dunmore Pottery at Airth, Stirlingshire, run by Peter Gardiner from about 1860 to 1903.

A punch bowl with an anti-Scottish theme. The figure of a Scotsman has his legs in the two compartments of a twin-seated privy. On the other side of the bowl is the rhyme:

> *When first to the South sly Sauney came forth,*
> *He was shewn to a place quite unknown in the North;*
> *That he is mistaken you soon will explore,*
> *Yet he Scratches and S--s as no man did before.*

Sauney is a version of Sandy or Alexander. The design is from a anti-Jacobite broadsheet first published in 1745, the year of the rising. It was published again in 1762, when feeling was high against Lord Bute, the Prime Minister and a Scotsman; and in 1779, when Bute was still suspected of influencing George III and the Catholic Relief Act had been passed.

The bowl was sold at Sotheby's in 1970 for £2000. It is 11¼ inches (28.5 cm) across. It was made in China for export to Europe.

Armorial Porcelain

How to keep up with the MacJoneses

A rich family in the eighteenth century often had the status symbol of porcelain specially made and decorated in China with the family's coat of arms. Armorial porcelain services for dinner, dessert, breakfast, tea, and coffee cost about ten times as much as ordinary ware from the East. The immense distance between Britain and China and the long time taken by ships on the voyage meant that an order took up to three years to arrive early in the century, although little more than a year by 1800.

About 20 percent of armorial porcelain was being made for Scots by 1745; but after the failure of the '45 the proportion dropped and many of the orders soon after that were for those who had supported the Hanoverian side. The proportion made for Scots rose again steadily and was about a quarter of all made between 1780 and 1800.

This lucrative business was part of the flourishing trade carried on with China by the East India companies of several European countries, especially Britain, Portugal, the Netherlands, Sweden, and Denmark. American vessels, too, were in the trade and became the largest buyers of porcelain after about 1815. Canton, the main port, was thriving and busy, sending out tea, silk, and other exotic goods as well as porcelain of all sorts.

Britain and Portugal had unusually voracious appetites for armorial porcelain. At least 4000 services were made for Britain alone between 1695 and 1820, most of them between 1715 and 1805; this means a service every six days during the eighteenth century.

Many of them were for marriages. A drawing of the coat of arms was sent off with the order. The strict rules of who was entitled to a coat of arms were from time to time ignored: people invented their own without the help of the College of Heralds in England or the Lord Lyon King of Arms in Scotland; or some used the arms of other families. On the other hand more scrupulous purchasers had a grant of arms before the order was placed—many of ancient origin.

Tragedy sometimes struck. A Swedish customer is said to have sent a sketch of his arms on a page torn from a school exercise book which had written on it: 'Mother is in an even worse temper than usual today.' This, the story goes, was faithfully reproduced on every item. Another design, of a British service, was sent with the colours labelled —'red', 'blue', and 'green'; again, the words appeared faithfully, under decoration of different colours. The Chinese could not be expected to understand the finer points of heraldry and because of incomplete instructions wrong colours were sometimes used. Armorial porcelain, made in European shapes and with European decoration, generally has a Chinese character about it.

Few documents about this trade have survived but an invoice of 1731 shows that the Peers family was charged £76 for a service of 500 pieces. Many services are still owned by the descendants of the original buyers, particularly in Scotland.

Chinese plate of the eighteenth century, 9 inches (23 cm) across and made for export. The decoration represents two soldiers of the 42nd Highland Regiment, later the Black Watch, who deserted for the Stuart cause in 1743. Three of them were executed in the Tower of London, and others were transported to Georgia; they became Jacobite martyrs. The figure on the right is Piper Macdonnel, one of those transported. The other figure is almost certainly one of those executed.

The Chinese artist has copied contemporary pictures of the martyrs.

Collectors tend to be of two sorts. The first sort is wealthy people who want showpieces and symbols of magnificence. (It is said that armorial porcelain is still used on grand occasions, but the nervous strain at washing-up time must be dreadful—and use damages the gilding.) The second sort is specialists who seek to get a variety of pieces showing different styles of known date which in turn can date porcelain without arms. Coats of arms on porcelain were large until about 1760, often filling the middle of a plate; but smaller after that. A knowledge of heraldry is valuable in tracking down the family if a coat of arms is unidentified. It also helps in approximate dating, for a family's arms often changed on marriage or death or elevation to a title.

This trade declined towards the end of the eighteenth century and died out by, say, 1820. Competition was growing from British and Continental factories. Imports had to pay very high duties. Wars endangered trade by sea. The enormous distance and delays were a burden. Efforts to cut costs of manufacture and make the wares more competitive meant that quality went down. 'Wrong' pieces are about, but not in great numbers. Genuine but non-armorial Chinese items of the eighteenth century have later been awarded coats of arms. Common items have been overpainted with rarer decoration in this century. A Parisian firm, Samson et Cie, made pseudo-Chinese ware during the nineteenth century and reproductions have been made in China during this century. Breakages have been replaced not from China but from British or Continental factories. The most desirable pieces are the earlier ones; chips and cracks reduce the value considerably.

China did a roaring trade with Europe during the eighteenth century in all sorts of porcelain made especially for European taste. The decoration includes masonic emblems, Jacobite or anti-Jacobite propaganda, Christian themes for Catholics or Protestants, mythological, erotic, or hunting scenes, and ladies and gallants. It must have been baffling for the craftsmen who worked half way round the world who had their own magnificent traditions in pottery and porcelain.

A punch bowl with the arms of Menzies of that Ilk of Castle Menzies. It is 14 inches (35.5 cm) across and was sold at Christie's in 1976 for £330.

Furniture

Comfortable, solid, and good value

The country lacked many of the things that make possible a splendid heritage in furniture, yet had its own distinguished makers, characteristic types, and style.

Many classes of society and many districts were comparatively poor; houses were small; even the larger houses had few pieces of furniture; little has come down to us from before 1700. The climate and the system of agriculture—expecially the destructive keeping of goats—meant that forests were few and trees stunted. Oak was a typically English material; beech, elm, and laburnum were typically Scottish. Pine and fir had to be imported from Scandinavia and oak from England; and mahogany came from the West Indies. The shortage of wood meant, however, that it was used with great care.

Wealthy patrons tended to buy their furniture from London or to buy, for example, one chair from London and have it copied nearer home—bulky goods had to be carried, at some cost, by sea. Fashion lagged behind London by perhaps 10 or 15 years. American fashion lagged in a similar way. One fine bureau-bookcase, for example, was thought to have been made in England about 1770; but it turned out to have the label of an Edinburgh maker and to date from 1809. Ordinary items for ordinary homes were made by joiners and house carpenters and are usually good and pleasing.

Fashionable English furniture is often stagey and elegant; the Scottish equivalent is more comfortable, heavy, and solid, and has the air of being good value for money. But identifying a piece as being definitely Scottish is all too often difficult. Absolute proof is possible only when accounts and furniture have survived together and this has happened rarely. Few makers put their names on their output with labels. The result is that genuinely Scottish furniture is unrecognised and in the course of the antique trade is likely to emigrate to other places. But much remains, and the documented pieces help to identify undocumented ones.

The Restoration of Charles II in 1660 brought some respite from strife but a more gracious manner of living did not arrive for perhaps 20 years. The style that was 'in' towards the end of the seventeenth century was not designed for much comfort. Chairs had high backs and were square or angular. Legs and other parts were often turned on a lathe to give a twisted appearance, like a stick of barley-sugar. Carved ornament was elaborate, even fussy. The beginning of the eighteenth century marked a change. Legs took on an elegant curve and are called cabriole legs. Backs of chairs were curved too, and fitted the body better. Several types of furniture were invented to suit a more gracious way of life.

Fashions were spread after the mid-eighteenth century by books of designs issued in London by the three most famous names in British cabinet making: Chippendale, Hepplewhite, and Sheraton. (Their historical order is, by chance, the alphabetical order of their names.)

Thomas Chippendale (1718–1779) published *The Gentleman and Cabinet-Maker's*

A sideboard in mahogany, of the late eighteenth century, 7 feet 7 inches (231 cm) wide. Typically Scottish is the gallery round the top. Sold at Sotheby's in 1976 to the Glasgow Museum and Art Galleries for £770.

Director in 1754. Other editions came out in 1755 and 1762 and among the subscribers to the later editions were several Edinburgh makers. The book gives designs for a wide range of items mainly in the rococo style which came from France: scrolls curved like the letters S and C, asymmetrical but balanced; rocks, shells, flowers, leaves, and icicles. Chippendale also gave designs in the Gothic, Chinese, and neo-classical style. Almost nothing is known of his personal life and some of the designs he published were by others. Nor was he the greatest cabinet maker of his time. But his name has become almost a household word because of the success of the *Director* and he did achieve great heights of artistry and craftsmanship. Anyone was free to copy his designs—that is why many craftsmen subscribed to the book. A piece of antique furniture modelled exactly on one of his designs may thus have been made by someone else. Many of the items unquestionably made by him were for houses designed by Robert Adam, a Scotsman and the most fashionable architect of his time.

George Hepplewhite (whose date of birth is unknown; he died in 1786). His designs were published after his death in *The Cabinet-Maker and Upholsterer's Guide*. They spread the neo-classical style, an attempt to reproduce the manner of the ancient world. Hepplewhite furniture is usually rectilinear, light, and elegantly proportioned. The backs of chairs are square, shield-shaped, or oval; and legs are tapered.

A pair of Cockpen chairs of the second half of the eighteenth century. The wood is mahogany. Reproductions of this type of chair are being made.

The *Guide* made it possible for ordinary middle-class homes to have good and fashionable furniture, and was calculated to be of service to 'Countrymen and Artizans, whose distance from the metropolis makes even an imperfect knowledge of its improvements acquired with much trouble and expence'.

Thomas Sheraton (1751–1806) was trained as a cabinet maker but earned his living as a teacher and author. His influential works were *The Cabinet-maker and Upholsterer's Drawing Book* (1791 to 1794) and *The Cabinet Dictionary* (1803). The *Drawing Book* was the more important. He also began his *Encyclopaedia* which started to appear in 1805 but by that time his mind was disordered and he was in abject poverty.

His style is an adaptation of the neo-classical and contemporary French styles. He liked sharp, simple lines, a rectilinear and slender appearance, fine proportions, and elegance. The explanations of his drawings were detailed and practical, and more than 600 makers, in London and outside London, were subscribers to the *Drawing Book*. Adam Black, a young man just arrived in London from Edinburgh, and 'seeking employment without success', worked for Sheraton in 1804 and wrote: 'He lived in an obscure street, his house half shop, half dwelling-house, and looked himself like a worn-out Methodist minister, with threadbare black coat. I took tea with them one afternoon. There were a cup and saucer for the host, and another for his wife, and a little porringer for their daughter. The wife's cup and saucer were given to me, and she had to put up with another little porringer . . . I was with him for about a week, engaged in most wretched work, writing a few articles, and trying to put his shop in order, working among dirt and bugs, for which I was remunerated with half a guinea. Miserable as the pay was, I was half ashamed to take it from the poor man'.

The greatest of Scottish cabinet makers was Alexander Peter of Edinburgh, who did work for—among others—the Duke of Argyll, the Countess of Hopetoun, and the Earl of Dumfries. The Earl began in 1754 to build himself a new house near Cumnock, Ayrshire, and went to London to buy furniture for it. He did some shopping at Chippendale's establishment in St Martin's Lane but also employed Peter—a typical instance of prudence and economy in the fitting out of a great Scottish house. His wife was dead and he was free to follow his own taste. Peter supplied Lord Dumfries with vast quantities of goods in 1757–1760. One of the items was a side table in mahogany copied exactly from the third edition of Chippendale's *Director*. This awareness of fashion was shown when Peter sent in his final account. Lord Dumfries wanted to return some chairs but Peter said that the fashion for chairs was changing every year and that out-of-date ones were not worth much. Peter did work for George Dundas of Dundas over a period of 11 years, at a total cost of £106 12s 2d (about £106.60). Some was paid in second-hand furniture and most of the rest in 163 bolls of meal worth £85 10s (£85.50).

Lord Dumfries also had work done by William Mathie of Edinburgh: a series of mirrors in the rococo and Chinese taste. They are spirited, even if they lack the technical brilliance of mirrors supplied to Lord Dumfries by Chippendale and Chippendale's partner, James Rannie. But Lord Dumfries wrote to his lawyer: 'Mr. Mathie has been extremely dilatorie and neglectfull in the execution of his

Commission which in a great measure prevents the furnishing of the House completely when the Upholsterers are in the House'.

Edinburgh was the biggest centre of furniture making in Scotland. The houses of the Old Town were cramped. Beds were sometimes disguised as something else during the day—for example they folded to look like cabinets. But building of the New Town—one of the most beautiful achievements of architecture and planning in the world—began in the 1760's. The gracious new streets, crescents, and squares demanded gracious furnishings.

William Brodie, a notorious profligate and burglar, was Deacon of the Incorporation of Wrights in Edinburgh and was a very competent cabinet maker. He inherited a thriving business from his father, Francis, who was for many years a member of the Town Council.

Deacon Brodie became addicted to gambling when he was young and went almost every night to a disreputable gaming-house in Fleshmarket Close. He formed a gang with three others, George Smith, Andrew Ainslie, and John Brown, and at the end of 1787 they committed a large number of burglaries in and around Edinburgh without being detected. They broke into the Excise Office off the Canongate on 5 March 1788. They were disturbed but the raid was carefully planned and they escaped with their booty.

Brown, who was under sentence of transportation for a crime committed in England, turned King's evidence. Brodie fled to Amsterdam and was about to go to the United States when he was caught. Brodie and Smith were hanged at the west end of the Luckenbooths in Edinburgh on 1 October, 1788. About 40,000 people watched.

The Brodies, father and son, had supplied furniture and done similar work for Edinburgh Town Council and Edinburgh University; the Deacon's fall gave a chance to Young and Trotter, a firm which was swiftly to gain pre-eminence among Scottish cabinet makers and to keep it for nearly 50 years. Its origins went back to at least 1671; the partners who founded its success were Robert Young and Thomas Trotter.

The firm moved in 1790 from the Luckenbooths to larger and more fashionable premises in Princes Street where the North British Hotel now is; and William Trotter became a partner. He created the 'Trotter' style—solid, of good workmanship, dignified, refined, and rather masculine. It is quite different from what was being made in London for the world of fashion. That furniture was often theatrical and impractical. Trotter did a great deal of work for the University: he was paid £1808 6s 3d (about £1808.31) in 1820 and £389 7s 8d (about £389.38) in 1824—substantial sums in those days. He redecorated and refurnished the Assembly Rooms and fitted up Parliament House in 1822 for the visit of George IV.

The firm excelled in a Scottish type of chair called a Cockpen chair. This has lattice work on the back which has a vaguely Chinese appearance and which needs considerable skill in fitting all the pieces of lattice together. The name was invented much later than the chairs: it seems to have come from some examples, which used to be in the Dalhousie family pew in the church at Cockpen, a village near Edinburgh. A leading scholar, Mr Francis Bamford, has written: 'Descended through his mother from a brother of the Reformer John Knox, William Trotter brought to the creation of fine furniture much of the energy, enthusiasm and obstinacy which characterised the great iconoclast.' Trotter became Master of the Merchant Company of Edinburgh in 1819 and was Lord Provost from 1825 to 1827. He bought the estate of Ballindean, Perthshire, and died in 1833.

His son took little interest in business and the firm went into decline. The tradition of furniture making in Scotland did not survive the mass production and the aberrations of taste in Victorian times.

Two Scots became leading cabinet makers in North America. Thomas Affleck, born in Aberdeen, went to Philadelphia in 1763, possibly from London. He excelled in Chippendale's version of Chinese, seems to have had a huge output, and died in 1795.

Duncan Phyfe (or Phyffe or Fife) was born in 1768 at Loch Fannich, Ross and Cromarty, and went with his parents to the United States in 1784. He was working in New York City by 1792 and became highly successful. He supplied the highest levels of society, sent goods to Philadelphia and the South, and may have had an agent in Baltimore. Phyfe used Sheraton's designs at the end of the eighteenth century and followed the British Regency and the French Directoire and Empire styles later. Most of his wood was mahogany from the Caribbean. Notable are his fine carving, restrained ornament, and good proportions. He died as late as 1843.

Clocks and Watches
Ingenuity and the search for accuracy

Most of our forefathers had only a vague idea of time because watches and clocks were expensive and generally inaccurate. Going about ordinary life and doing business must have been much less brisk and demanding. Watches did not become available to all until the end of the nineteenth century. Scientists have now devised timekeepers which depend upon the natural rhythm of the atom; caesium atomic clocks err by one second in 150,000 years. 'Leap seconds' as well as leap years have been devised to compensate for the erratic motion of the earth.

Traditional clocks are basically of two sorts: *bracket,* to stand on a shelf or a table; and *long case* or *grandfather*, to stand on the floor. Bracket clocks are driven by a coiled spring. Long case clocks are driven by weights which slowly descend—and that is why they have to be tall. More long case clocks were made in Britain than in any other country. The fashionable world of London was not keen on them after about the middle of the eighteenth century but they went on being made for ordinary customers and outside London.

Dials were first of brass and, from about 1770, of white and coloured paints treated by heat to make them permanent. Cases were of plain woods such as oak and mahogany; or veneered in walnut; or ornamented with marquetry; or japanned.

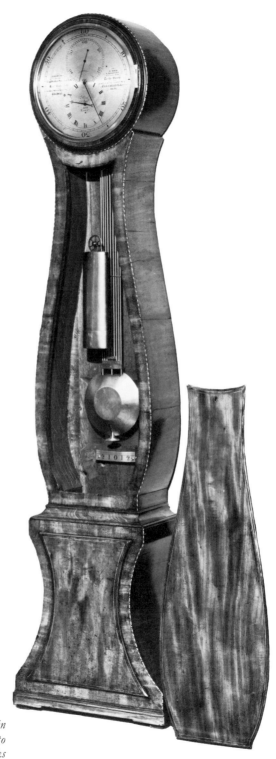

Clock made by Reid and Auld of Edinburgh in 1791. It is of the 'regulator' type—ie was made to keep particularly accurate time so that other clocks could be regulated against it.

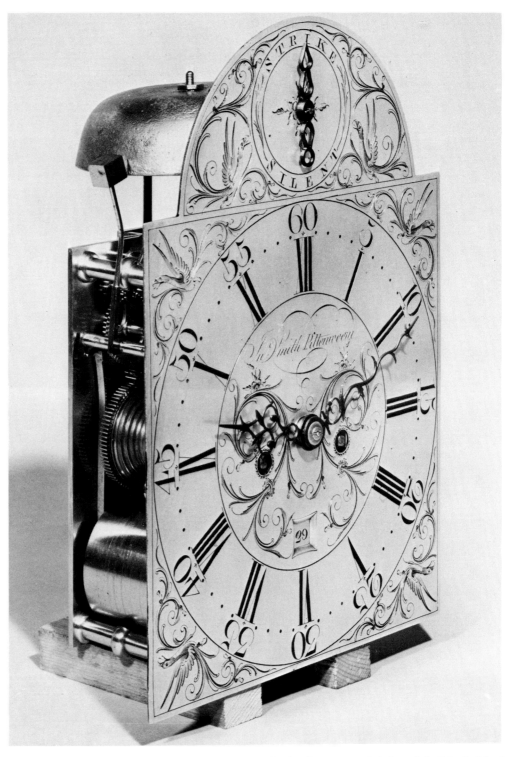

Dial and movement of clock made by John Smith of Pittenweem (1770–1814).

Watches were first made thick and large; the mechanism could thus be more easily designed for accuracy. But as the craftsmen achieved greater skills and better devices, watches became thinner and smaller. Dials were first made of silver or gilded metal raised up in a pattern or design and, from about 1725, of white enamel.

Scotland was comparatively slow in taking up the art and craft of making watches and clocks and usually tended to lag behind England in style and technology. But some makers excelled. John Smith (1770–1814), of Pittenweem, Fife, has been called a genius. His masterpiece was a long case or grandfather clock. It was seven feet high and the case was of mahogany. It chimed the quarters and hours and played a tune before the hour. It could play eight Scottish tunes, including Highland Laddie and Flowers of the Forest; a tune is played every three hours, and the clock can be made to play any of them at any time. The tempo can be changed to triple time. But all the music stops on the Sabbath and the words 'Remember Sunday' appear on the dial. Chimes can also be stopped for the night hours. This repertoire is not all. A dial on the side of the clock represents the front of a house. Inside the doorway is a figure of the macer of the Lords of Council and Session; he wears robes and carries a mace. When the clock plays he takes off his hat and walks past the door. He is followed by 15 Lords of Session in robes.

Clocks were being used in Scotland in the fourteenth century. One in St Mary's Church, Dundee, had become so worn and untrustworthy by 1540 that the town council made a contract with William Purves of Edinburgh for him to make 'ane sufficient and substantious knok [i.e. clock] with all instruments of iron work necessary and pertaining thereto, justly ganging [going] to strike hour and half hour complete and justly, the twenty-four hours day and night, with three warnings to contain six score and nine straiks [strokes], the first at four hours in the morning, the next at twelve hours at noon, and the third at nine hours at even [these were the times of matins, mass, and evensong] upon the five bells of the steeple, for the sum of seven score and seventeen pounds, ten shillings [Scots]'. This clock was set up on Palm Sunday, 1543. But Purves sued the town's officials over payment and the clock was destroyed by fire in 1553. Purves also worked on the clocks in Aberdeen and Stirling; he had great ingenuity and skill.

Aberdeen town council made a contract in 1453 with Johne Crukshanks to look after the clock for 60 shillings a year and he swore 'the great oath to do his delligent business to the keeping of it'. Aberdeen had some trouble with the clock in 1548. Robert Hoesoun was convicted of spoiling the clock and was ordered to mend it with the help of craftsmen 'and for the offence done the assize ordered him to come on Sunday come eight days and gang sark alane [i.e. wearing only a shirt], bare feet and bare leg, afore the procession with an candle of wax of ane pound weight in his hands, and there after to ask the provest and bailies forgiveness on his knees . . . and if he commit ony sick lik faut in time to comeing to be burnt on the cheek and banished the toun'.

Perhaps the most noted of Scottish clockmakers was David Ramsay, who had several offices under James VI and I: page of the bedchamber, groom of the privy chamber, and keeper of the clocks and watches. He also took out patents for ways of ploughing land, fertilising barren land, raising water by fire, propelling ships and boats, making saltpetre, manufacturing tapestry without a loom, refining copper, bleaching wax, separating gold and silver from base metals, dyeing fabrics, and smelting and refining iron by means of coal; but details of these inventions have not survived.

Ramsay was involved in an extraordinary incident recorded by William Lilly (1602–1681), an astrologer, prophet, and physician who dabbled in politics. Lilly wrote in his autobiography, the *History of Lilly's Life and Times*, that Ramsay had been told a great deal of treasure was buried in the cloister of Westminster Abbey. Ramsay, Lilly, and others went into the cloisters one winter's night; with them they had divining rods.

We played the hazel rods round about the cloisters. Upon the west end of the cloisters the rods turned over one another, an argument that the treasure was there. The labourers digged at least six feet deep, and then we met with a coffin; but which, in regard it was not heavy, we did not open, which afterwards much repented.

From the cloisters we went into the abbey church, where, upon a sudden, (there being no wind when we began,) so fierce and so high, so blustering and loud a wind did rise, that we verily believed the west end of the church would have fallen upon us. Our rods would not move at all; the candles and torches, also, but one were extinguished, or burned very dimly. John Scott, my partner, was amazed, looked pale, knew not what to think or do, until I gave directions and command to dismiss the demons; which, when done, all was quiet again, and each man returned unto his lodging late, about twelve o'clock at night. I could never since be induced to join with any such like actions.

The true miscarriage of the business was by reason of so many people being present at the operation; for there was about thirty, some laughing, others deriding us; so that, if we had not dismissed the demons, I believe most part of the abbey church would have been blown down.

Ramsay became Master of the Clockmakers' Company of London when it was incorporated in 1631. He fell into poverty in his later years. He was in prison for debt in 1641 when he petitioned the House of Lords for payment of six years arrears of his pension as groom of the privy chamber. He was given some money.

Sir Walter Scott introduced Ramsay as a character in *The Fortunes of Nigel*, but it is a fictional rather than factual portrait. Scott describes him 'an absent and whimsical man' with a 'tall, thin, lathy skeleton', lean jaws, and a yard-long face.

No Scottish watch or watchmaker is known by name from the death of David Ramsay until 1677 when the Incorporation of Hammermen admitted to their membership Paul Roumieu, a Frenchman who may have been a Huguenot fleeing from the persecution of the Protestants by Louis XIV. The Huguenots were a threat, Louis thought, to his power, and the Roman Catholic clergy were implacably hostile to the Huguenots. More than 400,000 Huguenots emigrated, many of them to Britain or Prussia which were Protestant, and took their skills with them. The persecution has been called one of the most flagrant political and religious blunders in the history of France. Roumieu, a highly skilled craftsman, was given special favours by the Hammermen. His watches are now extremely rare. Roumieu died in 1694 and was buried in the Greyfriars' churchyard,

Edinburgh. His son, also Paul, was a watchmaker in Edinburgh and at least two of his assistants were probably Frenchmen.

Clockmakers had become proficient by the middle of the eighteenth century. Long case clocks made outside London often tended to be comparatively broad and squat towards the end of the eighteenth century. Marquetry (inlaid wood) and japanning (lacquer) were done on the cases. Dials were also painted by artists: customers on the coast of Fife, for example, liked pictures of ships and fishing boats on their clocks.

Craftsmen trained in Edinburgh frequently set up business on their own in other towns but most of them are merely names in advertisements of the time. One watchmaker, for example, had this put in the *Edinburgh Gazette* in 1799:

James Barrow, aged about 20, of a low stature. a little pock-marked, speaks the English accent, had on when he went away a short flaxen coll cut wig, in an ordinary habit; run away from his master . . . with a plain gold watch without a christal . . . a silver pendulum watch . . . a plain silver watch and an oval brass watch, with several other things. Whoever can secure the said youth and give notice thereof to Captain Andrew Brown, watchmaker in Edinburgh, shall have two guineas reward.

An advertisement in the *Caledonian Mercury* of 12 October 1782 said:

Gold watch made by Roumieu of Edinburgh. It is dated 1699.

On Thursday, the 10th of October curt., there came to Stirling a young man who called himself William Colquhoun, and said he was a youth of landed property near Greenock, but a minor, and that a gentleman in the west country whom he named was one of his tutors, and that when at home he lived with the said gentleman. He bought a new watch from George Hutchison, watchmaker, Stirling, the maker's name, Robt. Innes, London, No. 6972, a bar movement with a sham repeating pendant, with a common steel chain and key, but the young man made his elopement without paying the watch or tavern bill. He was dressed in a drab duffle big coat, a blue undercoat and vest with yellow metal buttons, black breeches, and boots. He is dark complexioned, black hair, a large cocked hat. He rides on a small brown horse or mare inclining to a switch tail. It is entreated that all watchmakers, jewellers, or others who may see the said watch may stop the same and inform the Publishers or the said George Hutchison, watchmaker in Stirling. N.B.—It has been since found out that he goes by different names, particularly that of William Gairdner.

Advertisements in newspapers of the eighteenth century show that many of the watches in Scotland were made in London: and that watch and clock makers also depended for their livelihoods on retailing London goods, doing repairs, and selling kindred products such as small items of jewellery.

The trade does not seem to have been well advanced as late as 1784, when an advertisement in the *Caledonian Mercury* spoke of an undertaking 'to establish on an extensive plan all the necessary branches of watchmaking in Scotland'. The advertiser, William Falconer of Laurencekirk, Kincardineshire, added that he made 'the materials which used formerly to come from England . . . silver watches to be offered as low as two pounds after the period of three years . . . One half of the subscription money is to lie in a banker's hand so that, in case of . . . failure, subscribers cannot lose half their money'. He hoped the public would 'see the propriety of supporting his undertaking, as the manufacture of watches and all their materials in Scotland could not fail of saving and bringing much money to the country and giving bread to industrious mechanics ready to execute this undertaking'.

Clocks and watches which appear to be Scottish because they bear a Scottish maker's name and town may in fact be English: the name is of a retailer only. This time-honoured practice still goes on.

Scientific Instruments
For learning, use, and amusement

Machines can be beautiful. Old scientific instruments can also tell a story, be highly decorative, and do the job they were first intended for.

The making of such instruments was slow to start and was done mostly in Glasgow and Edinburgh. This was because the country had at first no great demand; and even when demand began to rise in the early decades of the eighteenth century many customers continued to turn to London, a centre of instrument making with an international reputation. But all sorts of instruments

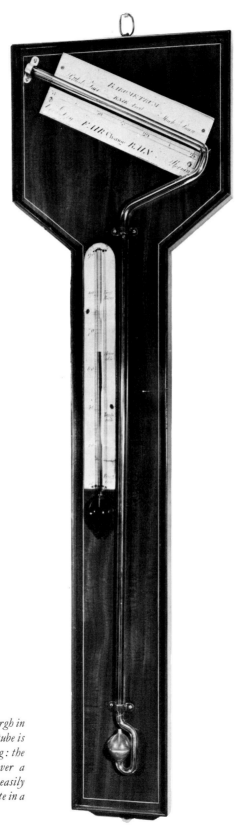

Barometer made by Balthazar Knie of Edinburgh in about 1800. Knie was of German origin. The tube is sloped at the top to give a more accurate reading: the movement of the mercury there is spread over a longer section of tube and can thus be more easily observed. But the shape is difficult to incorporate in a pleasing design.

did come to be made: sextants and octants (for navigation), sundials, barometers, hydrometers (for measuring specific gravity), thermometers, mirrors for telescopes, lenses for telescopes and microscopes, balances for testing coins, globes of the earth and sky, and so on.

A mathematician and compiler of almanacks James Corss, who has was born in Glasgow, complained in 1662: 'I have oftentimes lamented with myself to see so many Learned Mathematicians to arise in sundry parts of the world, and so few to appear in our Native Country. In other things we are parallel with (I shall not say in a superlative degree far above) other Nations; but in Arts and Sciences Mathematical, all exceed us. And had not that thrice Noble and Illustrious Lord, viz John Lord Nepper, Baron of Merchiston, &c. preserved the honour of our Nation by his admirable and more than mortal invention of Logarithms, we should have been buried in oblivion, in the memories of Forraign Nations'.

'Nepper'—the name is spelled in several ways—was John Napier (1550–1617) of Merchiston, now part of Edinburgh. He was born when his father was sixteen years old, went to St Andrews University, took part in theological disputation, lived as a laird, and had constant trouble with neighbours. He seemed to have devised two sorts of burning mirrors, a piece of artillery, and a metal chariot, armoured against muskets, whose motion was controlled by the people inside it and from which shots could be fired through small holes.

Pocket globe made by John Miller of Edinburgh in about 1793. The case shows the heavens with the larger stars.

His great invention of logarithms was published in 1614: it had enormous influence and revolutionised methods of computation in astronomy and scientific navigation. He also gave to the world a system of calculation by little rods, usually made of bone or ivory, called 'Napier's bones'. They were used for multiplication and division and could help in working out quite complex problems. Napier's bones, mostly made in the seventeenth century, are very rare and costly; Scottish-made examples are almost unknown.

The customers who did purchase scientific instruments from about 1700 onwards were scientists who needed special apparatus for research; professional people who used such things as theodolites (for surveying land) and octants (for navigation); and the cultured amateurs who bought sundials, microscopes, and similar objects for amusement as well as use. A very beautiful microscope made in Paris in about 1750 of costly materials and designed in the elaborate and fashionable rococo style was sold by Sotheby's in Monaco in 1976 for 350,000 French francs (£41,700). It is said to have been presented by Louis XV to Madame de Pompadour. Among the equipment for it is a slide imprisoning a louse. This microscope is of interest more as a beautiful object with glamorous associations than as a scientific instrument.

Microscopes were nevertheless valuable for the amateur scientist in the eighteenth century; and in the 1820s major advances were made in their optical systems.

An advertisement in the *Glasgow Courant* of 22 August 1755 said that John Carlile of Glasgow sold 'Silver Table Spoons, Tea Spoons and Tongs; Silver

Shoe-Buckles . . . Silver Spurs . . . Complete Sets of Tea-China . . . Fine Violins . . . Quadrants . . . complete Sets of Mathematical and Surgeons Instruments . . . Backgammon-Tables . . . Telescopes, Microscopes . . . Thermometers . . . Pomatum . . . Gauze Handkerchiefs . . .'

Advertisements in the *Caledonian Mercury* of 25 January 1773 and the *Glasgow Journal* of 11 February 1773, about a microscope, said: 'The curious are . . . well acquainted with the many surprising discoveries which have been made by means of it . . . whoever is a stranger to these, has a plentiful source of entertainment still before him, a new world in which he may expatiate with particular pleasure.' This instrument was by John Clark of Edinburgh, a goldsmith, jeweller, and optician. The advertisements show how the makers were seeking out the amateurs as buyers.

James Watt (1736–1819), who developed the steam engine beyond recognition as a major source of power for the Industrial Revolution, was at a crucial point in his career a maker of scientific instruments and worked at Glasgow University. He repaired for the University a model of the early steam engine designed by Newcomen; and when doing this realised how its poor performance could be improved. His invention—the separate condenser—was patented in 1769. Watt also discovered the composition of water and invented a micrometer and a machine for the copying and reproduction of sculpture. His skill with his hands, apparent in the early part of his career when he made instruments, was invaluable in much of his later work.

Demand for luxury goods went up towards the end of the eighteenth century. By the beginning of the nineteenth the makers of scientific instruments in Scotland were skilled and numerous enough to do quite demanding work for the professional scientists. William Thomson, later Lord Kelvin (1824–1907), one of the founders of modern physics, was offered the Chair of Experimental Physics at Cambridge in 1870 but refused it. One of his reasons was 'the convenience of Glasgow for getting mechanical work done'.

Names of makers to look out for are: Adie, a firm which started in Edinburgh in 1823 and changed its name from time to time (Adie and Son; Adie and Wedderburn); John Gardner of Glasgow, who learned his skills with James Watt and worked from about 1769 to 1792; James Short who worked in Edinburgh from 1734 to 1738 and moved to London—he was the great maker of reflecting telescopes; John Dunn of Edinburgh who worked from 1824 to 1842 and had a branch in Glasgow; John Dunn's brother Thomas, also of Edinburgh; Richard Griffin of Glasgow (mid-nineteenth century); James White of Glasgow, from 1850, who worked with Lord Kelvin; John Ramage of Aberdeen and his son, also John (they worked from 1806 to the 1830s); and George Lowdon of Dundee from 1850 onwards. Anything made by James Watt is bound to be very valuable.

Brass on instruments should be cleaned with a gentle type of polish, not an abrasive one. Taking instruments to pieces can be tricky for the amateur. Instrument makers' screwdrivers should be used; ordinary ones can do damage. It is unwise to dismantle an entire piece and then put it together: a better way is to dismantle and reassemble the piece bit by bit.

Finding out facts about a clock, watch, or scientific instrument or its maker is not simple; but the Royal Scottish Museum in Edinburgh gives advice, has a good collection, and keeps records of the makers to supplement the books of reference.

Quaichs

and their relations the bickers, coggies and luggies

Quaichs were very common drinking vessels. The word comes from the Gaelic 'cuach', meaning cup, but they were made and used in the Lowlands as well as the Highlands. Tobias Smollet wrote in his novel *Humphrey Clinker*, published in 1771:

When the Lowlanders want a chearupping cup, they go to the public house, called the Change-house, and call for a chopin [a measure] of twopenny, which is a thin yeasty beverage, made of malt; not quite so strong as the table-beer of England. This is brought in a pewter stoop, shaped like a skittle [i.e. a tappit hen, see page 29], from whence it is emptied into a quaff [i.e. quaich]; that is, a curious cup made of different pieces of wood, such as box and ebony, cut into little staves, joined alternately, and secured with delicate hoops, having two ears or handles. It holds about a gill, is sometimes tipped around the mouth with silver and has a plate of the same metal at bottom, with the landlord's cipher engraved.

Quaichs were also made from solid wood, hollowed out, and—rarely— in stone, horn, pewter, brass, and bell metal (an alloy of copper and tin). They vary in size, in spite of Smollet saying they held about a gill. Most had two handles or lugs but a few had three or four.

A silver quaich made in Edinburgh in 1665–1667. The bowl is 6 inches (15.2 cm) across and the lugs are 9½ inches (23.3 cm) across. It has the marks of the maker, Alexander Reid the second, and of the deacon, James Symountoun.

Silver mounts were often added to wooden quaichs in the seventeenth century and towards 1700 the whole object was often made in silver. The quaich is still popular for prizes. But Sir James Foulis of Colinton wrote in 1792: 'There can hardly be a person that knows it not, though it is of late much fallen into disuse'.

A type of vessel akin to the quaich is the bicker, which was also made in varying sizes. Bickers have straight sides and are shaped rather like buckets. They are made of staves of dark and light wood: the light is generally sycamore and the dark is alder which has been steeped in peat to make it turn a dark brown. The whole is held together by eight or nine bands of willow. Great skill was needed in fitting the staves exactly together so that they are neat and water-tight. Two staves, always of light-coloured wood, are extended upwards and outwards to form handles. Some bickers have double bottoms with a pea in the space between them; this was so that a drinker could make a rattling noise when he wanted more liquor. Small bickers were for whisky or other spirits; medium sized ones for ale or for food such as porridge; and really large ones (called cogs or coggies) were for a communal meal of porridge or for large quantities of ale.

Luggies are wooden vessels with one lug or handle; keelers are large, oval, shallow pans for cooling milk. All these vessels are rare.

COINS AND TOKENS

Coins

A window into history

A medical man once gave a patient a prescription and told him to take it to a firm of coin dealers. It said that the patient was to start collecting and even suggested an area for him to specialise in. Coins, apart from their therapeutic value as a hobby, are of exceptional interest for several reasons. They are often the only objects made in some remote period that can be bought by ordinary collectors. Very many of them now surviving were at one time hidden in the ground or in buildings, especially when people were in danger from war or robbers. Moreover they can be of exceptional aesthetic or historic interest. Some Scottish coins of the Renaissance are superb; the town of Berwick was sometimes occupied by the Scots and sometimes by the English, and these changes can be traced in the coins that were struck there.

Mediaeval Scottish coins as a whole are very difficult to study and even now much scholarly work has still to be done. They were often poorly made or poorly designed and that adds to the difficulties. They are costlier than the English because they are rarer: the ratio of Scots to English is about one to twenty.

A remarkable rise in the price of almost all coins happened at the end of the 1950s. People seemed to be more and more interested in the past and beautiful things of the past. More wealth was about to be spent on 'luxuries'. Increases in prices attracted investors.

All this meant that coins were scarcer and harder for collectors of modest means to buy. Great collections were formed in the last century and the first half of this century but could not be formed today. Numismatists may now have to travel around the country to see coins in museums rather than have them in their own homes.

Condition is of the first importance. A code is used to describe it.

FDC: is fleur-de-coin; perfect in every way.

UNC: uncirculated and as issued by the Mint but, because of mass production not necessarily perfect.

EF: extremely fine. Shows little signs of wear but with small marks on the surface when examined very closely.

VF: very fine. Slight traces of wear because of slight circulation.

F: fine. Considerable wear. Or perhaps the design is weak because of poor striking.

Fair: worn but with the main features and the inscription still distinguishable. Or very poorly struck.

Poor: very worn indeed and of no interest to collectors unless it is extremely rare.

Subtle shades of difference between these grades are often indicated, such as 'almost extremely fine'.

Names given to the different denominations are unfamiliar to modern eyes. The crown and half crown are the lion and demy-lion or demy: one side of the coin has a lion. The rider gets its name from its figure of the king on horseback, in armour and with a drawn sword. The unicorn has the animal with a shield and the bonnet piece (or ducat) is named from the bonnet on the king's head. Other denominations are the plack, groat, bawbee, turner, bodle, ryal, pistole, and testoon. Many of these varied in value from time to time as the coinage was debased or restored.

David I (1124–1153) encouraged Anglo-Norman families to settle in the country, promoted English influence, and helped the advance of the English language. He was the first king to issue coins; the people had until then used the issues of, for example, the Northumbrian and English kingdoms and of the Vikings. English coins circulated for centuries after the Scottish coinage was well established. David's coinage imitated that of Stephen, king of England, in standard of silver, types of coin, and even the slovenly craftsmanship.

Malcolm IV (1153–1165) was called the 'Maiden' because he succeeded to the throne when he was only 12. He died unmarried. His coins are extremely rare.

William I (1165–1214) was named the Lion because he put the lion rampant on the Scottish arms, replacing the dragon. He was captured by the English in 1174 and had to pay homage for the whole of Scotland to the English king and hand over the castles of Roxburgh, Berwick, Edinburgh.

Paying homage was a crucial issue in Scotland's fight for independence; but the submission of William the Lion was later annulled. Richard I of England, needing all the money he could lay his hands on for the Crusades, sold back the independence of Scotland in 1189 for 10,000 marks. This would represent 1,600,000 silver pennies but was probably to be paid in bullion rather than coins.

Alexander II (1214–1249) came to the throne when he was 16. The kingdom was continually afflicted with troubles because so many of the sovereigns succeeded when they were young. Alexander sided with the English barons against King John at the time of Magna Carta. Coins were struck in the name of William the Lion for perhaps 20 years after he died. Coins of Alexander II are exceptionally rare.

Coins of *Alexander III* (1249–1286) are the commonest of the mediaeval period in Scotland. Mints were at Roxburgh, Perth, Aberdeen, Edinburgh, Inverness, St Andrews, Kinghorn, Lanark, Berwick, and several other places. His reign was prosperous. The Norsemen were forced to yield control of the Western Isles, keeping only Orkney and Shetland. But the end was darkened by tragedy: his sons died and he was killed when he and horse, travelling in darkness, fell over a cliff.

Penny of Alexander III (1249–1286). Alexander came to the throne when he was seven and died when he was 44 when he and his horse fell over a cliff in darkness.

Four penny piece or groat of Robert III (1390–1406). He was almost totally disabled by an accident before he came to the throne and power was in the hands of his younger brother Robert Stewart, Duke of Albany.

Groat of James VI, made in Edinburgh.

Margaret, the Maid of Norway, was aged three when she succeeded but she never set foot in her kingdom and no coins of her reign are known.

Edward I of England, who considered himself 'Lord Paramount' over Scotland, chose from many contenders for the succession *John Baliol* (1292–1296) who ruled as a vassal of England but who renounced his fealty. Edward invaded and sent Baliol to England and then France. The wars meant that hoards of coins were buried for safety and turned up again many years later. English governors ruled for 10 years but the country was in rebellion. John Baliol's coins were of the same type as Alexander III's.

Robert Bruce (1306–1329) gradually drove out the English. It is likely that Alexander III's issues were still being made, for Robert Bruce's coins with his own name are rare. Edward Baliol, son of John Baliol, was a pretender to the throne and was supported by Edward III of England. He was crowned at Scone in 1332 but was finally driven out by barons loyal to Robert Bruce's son David in 1338. No coins of his are known.

David II (1329–1371) was five when he came to the throne and spent seven years of his childhood in France because the English were again ravaging the country. He was captured by the English in 1346, spent seven years in captivity, and was ransomed for 100,000 marks: a sore burden on the country but never paid in full. It was during his reign that the first attempt was made at a gold coinage. This was a noble, worth six shillings and eight pence, or half a Scottish mark. It followed closely in design the noble of Edward III of England and carried for the first time the lion rampant. Round the edge is the inscription: IHC AUTEM TRANSIENS PER MEDIUM ILLORUM IBAT ('But Jesus passing through the midst of them went his way', Luke IV, 30). The text had a strong magical flavour in the Middle Ages; the hope was that being round the edge of the coins it would be a discouragement to clipping.

Testoon of Mary Queen of Scots, 1557.

Robert II (1371–1390), the first of the Stewart line, was a feeble ruler. His coins have little interest or significance.

Robert III (1390–1406) was almost totally disabled by an accident before he became king. A regular gold coinage was begun, the lion and half-lion ('demy'); but towards the end of the reign all coins were made lighter. Silver was scarce.

James I (1406–1437) had been captured by the English before his father Robert III died and he was their prisoner until 1424: his ransom was £40,000. He was well educated, was a poet and scholar, reduced the power of the magnates, and

Thirty shilling coin of James VI, 1582: a handsome design.

believed wealth depended on a good quantity of coined money. Taxes were put on the export of gold and silver. Exports of wool, cloth, hides, and fish had to pay taxes in silver bullion. The main coins were the demy in gold and the groat, worth sixpence, in silver.

James II (1437–1460). A new coinage was ordained in 1451. It was to be kept in theory to the standard and weight of corresponding English issues but in fact was less good. Within a few years new and higher values were decreed for the coins—a quick profit for the Crown. James was killed by the explosion of a cannon during the siege of Roxburgh Castle.

Some pennies and farthings were issued during the second half of the fifteenth century by a non-royal mint. The pennies were probably made under the authority of the Bishop of St Andrews but the farthings' origin is unknown. A great hoard of these and other coins was discovered in 1919 at Crossraguel Abbey, Ayrshire, in the bed of a stream that flushed the latrines.

James III (1460–1488). The state of the country was at times desperate and this was reflected in farthings of copper—the first coins struck in copper in the British Isles in mediaeval times. A thistle was first used on coins as a national emblem. The face of James III depicted on one type of groat is the first true portrait in the Scottish coinage and is probably the earliest Renaissance portrait to appear on a coin outside Italy.

James IV (1488–1513). Forgery was a problem* and some were struck 'sa subtillie and in sik forme of mettle that it is unpossible to discern and know the trew fra the fals'. A new coinage was planned but the king and the flower of Scotland's chivalry were killed at Flodden. The state of the currency tended at this time to be bad and this, together with the 'gret wer betwix Scotland and Ingland . . . causyt baith hungar and derth, and mony pur folk deit of hungar'.

---

*Henry I of England decided in 1124 to punish the moneyers (supervisors of mints), according to the Anglo-Saxon Chronicle. 'Bishop Roger of Salisbury sent all over England, and commanded them to assemble at Winchester by Christmas. When they came thither they were then taken, one by one, and each deprived of the right hand and the testicles below. All this . . . was entirely justified because they had ruined the whole country by the magnitude of their fraud.'

Thirty shilling piece of Charles I, made between 1637 and 1642. The craftsman was Nicholas Briot, a Frenchman who was extremely skilled but whose appointment as Master of the Scottish mint annoyed other officials. He used new machinery.

A merk of Charles II, 1671.

James V (1513–1542). This reign is notable for the first Scottish coin to carry a date. It is a ducat or 'bonnet piece'—because the king is shown wearing a bonnet. These ducats were minted in gold from Crawford Muir and Corehead.

Mary Queen of Scots (1542–1567) had one of the most romantic and tragic histories of all the monarchs. She was only a few days old when her father died. She was sent to live at the French court when she was five (her mother was French) and she married the son of the French king in 1558 when she was 18. Her father-in-law was killed in a tourney the next year and she became Queen of France. But she was a childless widow in little more than a year and she went back to Scotland.

Religious reformers were becoming stronger. Mary married her cousin Henry, Lord Darnley, in 1565; he was murdered mysteriously in 1567 and she was suspected of having a hand in the affair. They had had one son, the future king of Scotland and England. Mary then married James Hepburn, Lord Bothwell. Rebellion overthrew her and she fled to England, 18 years of captivity, and execution by the axe on the orders of Elizabeth. The changes in the Queen's life are reflected in the coins. Some issues in silver, of 1561–1562, have a beautiful portrait of her. Its inspiration is said to have been a painting by Francois Clouet, a French artist. Other issues have much less flattering portraits even when she was young and pretty. Forgeries were rife again. Some came from abroad, especially Flanders. A coiner was liable to be hanged, drawn, and quartered, or strangled and burnt at the stake, or if the verdict was more lenient simply hanged.

James VI and *I* of England (1567-1625), the 'wisest fool in Christendom', received a first class education but had a deeply flawed personality. He never knew his mother. The two kingdoms were united because Elizabeth was unmarried and produced no heirs, but Scotland retained her own Parliament and administration. Civil strife over religion was to continue almost to the end of the seventeenth century. James's coins were issued in many forms and one reason was his regular shortage of funds. He could literally make money for himself by issuing coins at a face value greater than the worth of the metal. The Scottish currency was steadily devalued in relation to the English—by 1390 it was worth half; by 1475–1544 a quarter; by 1579 one eighth, and by 1603, when the crowns were united, one twelfth.

Coins had to be called in for the sake of their metal and this means that many types are rare. The people were afflicted by a confusing mass of different issues. But the reign did produce some exceptionally beautiful specimens. One authority, Mr Ian Stewart, has written: 'It would not be an idle claim to say that no single period in the history of any country has left more beautiful art treasures in its coins than the second half of the sixteenth century in Scotland . . . The English coins, gold especially, were imposing and majestic, the French were delicate and pretty. Scotland finds perfect harmony between the two'.

If the King made a profit, so could the forgers—and forgery was widespread. A certain Thomas Peebles was hanged and his limbs and head torn from his body and put on public show.

Among splendid specimens from this period are the £20 gold piece of 1575 and 1576 and the thistle nobles or Scottish rose-nobles of 1588–1590.

Charles I (1625–1649) and the Commonwealth (1649–1660): wars over the constitution and religion. A very large variety of coins was issued. Nicholas Briot, a Frenchman, was specially appointed by the king as master of the Scottish mint in 1635. He used a new type of machinery, the mill and screw, and produced thus many exquisite pieces. Other officials were jealous and hampered him. Huge quantities of copper coins were struck in the first half of the seventeenth century, for example in 1650. No coins were struck in Scotland during the Commonwealth after that.

Charles II (1660–1685). Religious strife continued. The king was crowned at Scone in 1651 but his reign did not start for another decade. Coins were no longer hammered but were made by the press; this meant that they were more uniform in size. The mint was closed from 1682 to 1687 because high officials were prosecuted for improper or corrupt behaviour.

James VII and *II* of England (1685–1689) was a Roman Catholic and was deposed. Only 40-shilling and 10-shilling pieces were struck.

William II and *III* of England (1689–1694): Protestant succession. The massacre at Glencoe is a dark page in his reign. The most interesting coins were £6 and £12 pieces of 1701 from gold dust bought by the Darien Company from Africa. The aim was to keep bullion in the country. The company was to make a profit because the coins were 10 percent lower in gold content than their face value. This profit was, however, considerably reduced because the gold was below standard and had to be refined at some expense.

Anne (1702–1714). The last Stuart sovereign. The last native Scottish coins to be minted in Scotland were 10 shilling and 5 shilling pieces of 1705 and 1706.

The Treaty of Union of 1707 created a united Parliament and laid down that 'the coin shall be of the same standard and value throughout the United Kingdom as now in England, and a Mint shall be continued in Scotland under the same rules as the Mint in England'. Recoinage of the Scottish money was carried out by the Mint in Edinburgh and the task was finished quickly: the issues dated 1709 were the last official coins struck in the country. The Coinage Act of 1870 prohibited the making of coins except by the English Mint—one of many breaches of the 1707 Act.

James VIII (The Old Pretender), son of James VII and a Roman Catholic, attempted an invasion in 1708 to recover the throne and did land and lead a rising in 1715. He planned a currency. Dies were made for a crown piece dated 1709; only one specimen is known to have survived. Dies were also made for a coinage dated 1716—guineas and crowns. No coins are known to have been struck at the time but the dies came into the hands of a London dealer, Matthew Young, who struck specimens from them in 1828. The dies were then defaced.

Emblems such as the Scottish lion, Scottish crown, thistle and cross of St Andrew have been put on some modern British coins.

Bank Notes

Money that still has value

A millionaire was once asked if he spent any of his fortune on collecting and replied: 'Yes, I collect banknotes . . .' That was before the birth of a comparatively new hobby—notaphily, or the collecting of paper money in the same way as stamps or coins.

Anyone can become a multi-millionaire, on paper, by acquiring notes issued in times of grotesque inflation. An example is one issued in Hungary in 1946 with a value of 100,000,000,000,000,000 pengoe. Banknotes are often footnotes to history and can tell the story of wars, sieges, revolutions, fraud, forgery, and the prosperity or poverty of ordinary people.

Scottish notes are of special interest: in no other country did they contribute so much to the economy during the eighteenth and nineteenth centuries. The Scottish banks collapsed from time to time, but their creditors were always paid in full. Their notes remained valid. English private banks, on the other hand, appeared and disappeared like mushrooms and when they did collapse their notes became worthless. No fewer than 525 English banks failed in 1772. Notes of a broken English bank were worthless as money but were sometimes kept as souvenirs. That is why they still turn up and are collectable. But Scottish notes from failed Scottish banks were cashable and so rarer—at least the early ones. The very first Scottish notes were issued by the Bank of Scotland in the 1690s. They were in pounds Scots: twelve pounds Scots being the equivalent of one pound sterling. The Treaty of Union created a single currency for Britain, but people in Scotland tended to think in the old currency. Burns wrote that the 'cutty sark' or short petticoat of the pretty young witch in *Tam o'Shanter* cost 'twa pund Scots', and the poem dates from 1791.

A huge variety of issues appeared over the years; now only three banks are producing their own. Bankruptcy or amalgamation saw the end of the local ones in Arbroath, Caithness, Dumfries, Dundee, Greenock, Kilmarnock, Montrose, Paisley, Perth, Stornoway, and dozens of other places. A craze broke out in the eighteenth century for the issuing of notes by individuals and by traders such as grocers and licensed victuallers. Some were for as little as one shilling Scots (one old penny sterling). Anyone had the right to do it and all that was needed was someone to be willing to accept the note. These were not banknotes and are in any case rare, but are valuable.

Antique specimens are often different from the ones we are used to. They are printed on one side only; the blank side gave scope for graffiti such as religious texts, political slogans, and ribald rhymes. Officials of the banks signed the notes. The left hand side may appear to be incomplete but this is not a defect. Each one had a counterfoil from which it was taken when it was issued; it could later be checked against the counterfoil. Most examples dating from before 1853 have an embossed or printed stamp to show that duty had been paid on it. The duty was another reason why old Scottish specimens are scarce: withdrawing the note meant that the amount paid in duty was lost. The prudent Scottish bankers tried to keep their issues in circulation as long as the paper hung together.

Forgeries existed but do not seem to have been as great a problem as in England. Eight people were executed in Scotland for forgery between 1806 and 1825; more than 300 were executed in England in the same period. The Scottish banks gave cash for forged notes so that confidence was maintained.

Guarding against forgery was done by making the designs and the engraving more and more elaborate and careful. Collectors have benefited too because many of the examples from 1825 to 1860 are real works of art. Some of the spurious examples were made by soldiers and sailors who were captured during the wars

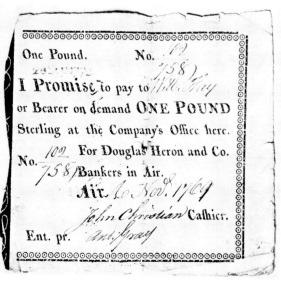

Pound note of Douglas Heron and Co, the Air (Ayr) Bank—a rare specimen. It is 5¼ inches (13½ cm) wide. The bank was set up in 1769 and wound up in 1773. The failure was because of over-trading and irregularities but no crime was involved.

Original design for Royal Bank of Scotland £100 note, in pencil and red and black watercolour. This is for a type of note first issued in 1854. The design was sold at Christie's in 1976 for £385. The firm of W H Lizars did much engraving of notes for Indian, Canadian, American, Isle of Man, English, and Scottish banks; this design was from a collection of Lizars material which had descended through the family and was sold by auction.

against revolutionary France and Napoleon and who were kept in camps near Edinburgh and Perth. Their captors were probably in the racket too. (The prisoners also made money by producing and selling models of ships in wood and bone.)

A notaphilist has enormous scope elsewhere if he finds that Scottish notes tend to be hard to come by. Many people want to own specimens from the Ming dynasty (1368–1644) which were printed on paper made from the bark of mulberry trees. They look as if they are made of grey cardboard and are inscribed: 'Government note of the Ming Empire circulating for ever and ever'. They carry the warning that forgers will be beheaded and their property handed over to the person who denounces them. Ming notes succumbed to inflation but are nowadays what you might call the Ming vases of notaphilists. Other prized items are the £1000 notes of the Bank of England. About 60 seem to be unredeemed but most are likely to have been lost or destroyed. Baden-Powell produced his own issues during the siege of Mafeking and Gordon during the siege of Khartoum.

Unissued £100 note of the City of Glasgow Bank,
nineteenth century. Worth about £850 in 1976.

Tokens

. . . or how to make do without real money

Currency has always been liable to abuse, as has been mentioned in the section about coins. It has often been forged in spite of horrendous legal penalties such as hanging and quartering. It has been clipped for the sake of getting the valuable metal. Governments have reduced the quality of silver and have devalued money by printing it in excessively large quantities. The last great debasement of the coin in Britain was in 1946 when silver was withdrawn and cupro-nickel issued instead. This was done to pay some of the vast amounts of money borrowed from the United States during the Second World War.

The British Government during most of the eighteenth and the early part of the nineteenth centuries neglected the coinage and the people suffered. Change was often in desperately short supply and made shopping awkward, especially for the poor. The Government issued only £1,500,000 worth of silver coins between 1716 and 1816—a pathetic trickle. Coins in circulation were often sorry-looking specimens. Lord Liverpool wrote at the end of the eighteenth century: 'Our present Silver coins are mere counters, without any impression on the face or reverse, or any graining on the edges, or indeed any exterior mark by which they can be distinguished as Coins'.

The Mint in London held aloof from issuing copper coins, which were not considered to be proper money at all: a base metal was unfit to be stamped with the monarch's head. Very little copper was struck in the reign of George III and none at all between 1775 and 1795. Employers were forced to pay their men in gold. But one man's weekly wages were almost certainly going to be less than a pound or a guinea so the workers were paid in pairs and had to split the money themselves. Lord Liverpool wrote that when wages were paid in an ale-house the men were tempted 'to spend, in the purchase of liquors, a part of what they have gained by their industry, which ought to have been reserved for the sober maintenance of themselves and their families'. Payment of wages in goods was another oppression of the poor if the value of the goods was set too high.

The silver coinage was dead towards the end of the eighteenth century, the copper was appallingly bad, and the gold was minted on a small scale. These gaps were partly filled by forgeries, tokens, foreign coins recruited into Britain's service, and bank notes.

Tokens were common in England in the seventeenth century. The diarist John Evelyn wrote in 1697 about the tokens 'which every taverne and tippling house ... presum'd to stamp and utter for immediate exchange ... they were payable through the neighbourhood ... though seldom reaching further than the next street or two'. All sorts of other businesses issued tokens. Scotland did not need them in the seventeenth century because it had its own copper currency—a mixed blessing, since its purpose was enriching the King as well as allegedly helping the people. But tokens were made in great numbers and varieties in the eighteenth and early nineteenth centuries. Bakers, grocers, publicans, tobacconists, seed merchants, mill owners, iron masters, town councils, and private individuals issued them. Some were intended for collectors at the time; and collectors nowadays like them because they are inexpensive, can be attractively designed, and have strong local associations. Most are from Edinburgh, Glasgow, and Dundee but many are from quite small places such as Duns (Berwickshire), Hawick (Roxburghshire), and Inverkeithing (Fife).

The shortage of silver was also eased by using Spanish 'dollars' which were eight-*real* pieces and roughly the size of a British crown piece. These were circulated at 4s 9d (about 24p). The Mint stamped them with the impression of the King's head (a similar stamp was put on objects made of silver to show that duty had been paid on it—see page 26). This gave rise to the sayings 'two kings'

A Spanish dollar of 1812 countermarked by the firm of J and A Muir of Greenock and circulated at a value of 4s 6d.

heads not worth a crown' and 'the Bank to make their dollars pass Stamped the head of a fool on the head of an Ass'. Some of the dollars were captured from Spanish treasure ships on their way from South America to Spain—great quantities of silver came from South American mines. The Battle of Cape Santa Maria in 1804, for example, resulted in the taking of three Spanish frigates, the sinking of another, and the enrichment of Britain by 2,028,216 dollars. It was really an act of piracy, for Britain and Spain were not then at war.

Scotland rather liked dollars stamped by merchants and industrialists, especially the owners of collieries and cotton mills. The stamp was generally circular with the name of the issuer and the value—for example, PAYABLE AT ALLOA COLLIERY 5/- and PAYABLE AT LANARK MILLS 5/-.

Other coins, British and foreign, were stamped, such as a United States dollar, a shilling of George III, a ½d of George III, and a bawbee of Charles II.

Eventually, when the Napoleonic Wars were over, the Government accepted its duty to provide the country with small change. Dollars with the King's head were withdrawn, and legislation was passed against tokens. Poor people left with the worthless tokens suffered quite serious losses.

Communion Tokens

A part of the way of godliness

The churches in Scotland used to issue worthy and godly folk with tokens to allow them to take communion, and these communion tokens are inexpensive to collect. They also give an insight into long-dead customs.

Left to right:
Auchterarder: OK for Ochterarder Kirk; Beith: AC for Associated Congregation; Contin: on reverse is date 1806.

Left to right:
Irvine: Relief Church 1840; Reverse of Parish of Buittle token, 1848. Table no. 6;

Left to right:
Aberdeen: John Knox Parish 1880; Perth: Arms of Perth; Montrose: Melville Church.

Left to right:
 Kinnoull: *1826; London: Liverpool Street, St Andrew's Church.*

Left to right:
 America: United Presbyterian, Dayton, Pen, 1969; Scotland: Wishaw Congregational 1966 (the latest known Scottish Communion token).

Tokens are small discs—up to 1½ inches (3.73 cm) across—and are generally of lead. They are also, but very rarely, of brass, tin, copper, iron, leather, and so on. They are square, oblong, round, triangular, or in other various shapes, and some are so badly made that they are almost shapeless.

Each one had to be unmistakably from a particular parish or congregation, to prevent imposters from getting to the communion table. Tokens thus have the initial letters of the parish, or the first letters of the parish, or its full name, or the minister's initials, or a picture of the church, or an emblem such as Dundee's pot of lilies or Edinburgh's castle, or the date (to prevent the use of old tokens).

Also found are a heart (to signify Christ's love for sinners); a sun (for the sun of righteousness); the communion cup, sometimes with the sacramental bread; a vine ('Christ is the true vine'); a fish. One writer said early this century: 'The fish was a very common symbol in early Christian art; it is frequently found in the Catacombs of Rome, but it is surprising to find it used in the Presbytery of Lerwick.'

Communion was usually held about once a year, but in some places only once in seven or nine years, from the end of the seventeenth century until about 1750. The people and the churches wanted to be sure they were ready for the sacrament. Gatherings were immense, and scandalous scenes sometimes took place between 1750 and about 1800. Each person had to get approval for each communion: the kirk session at Rhynd, Perthshire, declared in 1615 that 'the congregation repeat the shorter Catechezm as formerly, Lads among themselves two and two and the Lasses among themselves two and two'. In Lasswade, Midlothian, the minister decreed from the pulpit in 1710 that 'nane get tickats [tokens] but those that has bidden tryall and are fund weill instructit in the Belief, Lords Prayer, and Ten Commands.' Some people came from as far as 30 miles away, equipped with tokens from their own ministers. In Rutherglen, near Glasgow, a man was ordered in 1609 to appear before the Presbytery of Glasgow 'for his contemptuous sitting still at the Lordes table' when he was commanded by his minister 'to ryce thairfra'.

Tokens got worn out or lost or, if they had the minister's name, became obsolete when the minister moved. But they were treated with almost superstitious reverence because of their connection with the sacrament. Old ones were—rarely—buried beneath the pulpit; or they were melted to make new.

The makers were local blacksmiths, plumbers, or pewterers. Punches or dies were used to imprint the design; or molten metal was poured into stone moulds; or a copper coin was hammered out and the metal was crudely engraved by hand. But the old tradition almost died out towards the end of the Victorian period when printed cards came in. The tradition, however, went abroad: the Rev John Cuthbertson of the Reformed Presbyterian Church used tokens when he dispensed communion at Stony Ridge, Cumberland County, Pennsylvania, in 1752. Silver tokens were used by the Crown Court Chapel, London, and by the Presbyterian Church at Charleston, South Carolina. Ivory ones were used by the first Reformed Presbyterian Church, New York City.

Collecting these objects is made even more absorbing by the stories of the different churches. Tokens were not issued only by the Church of Scotland, but by many others. The Covenanters fought for half a century against having bishops, and thousands were fined, banished, imprisoned, tortured, or executed between 1638 and 1688. Their tokens were not only to sort out the godly from the ungodly but also to keep out Government spies. These examples are now the rarest and most valuable but all tokens of that time are rare. A full Covenanters' set might be worth several hundred pounds.

Reformed Presbyterians were the direct descendants of the Covenanters and at one time officially called themselves by the resounding title: 'The United Societies of the General Correspondences of the suffering Remnant of the true Presbyterian Church in Scotland'. Other Churches include the Secession and Relief Churches (these two formed the United Presbyterian Church in 1847), the original Secession, Free, Berean, Methodist, and Episcopal Churches—all of which issued tokens.

The system was used, too, in England and on the Continent and before the Reformation; but tokens were more widely used in Scotland than anywhere else.

Value depends on several things. The earlier they are the more valuable they are. Unusual shapes and pretty designs are desirable; corroded examples are not. Mrs May Sinclair of the dealers Spink and Son points out that people are turning to this field because coins and trade tokens (privately minted 'money') have become more and more expensive.

Robert Burns wrote a satirical poem on communion services, called Holy Fair and based on what he had observed in Mauchline, Ayrshire:

Here some are thinkan on their sins,
   An' some opo' their claes   (claes—*clothes*)
Ane curses feet that fyl'd his shins,   (fyl'd—*dirtied*)
   Anither sighs an' pray's.

Youths flirt with girls; a man puts his arm round his girl friend and lets his hand wander to her bosom; drinking goes on; preachers cant; gossip is about people's dress; assignations are made; and whores are present. He ends:

How monie hearts this day converts,
   O' sinners and o' Lasses!
Their heart o' stane, gin night are gane
   As saft as onie flesh is.
There's some are fou o' *love divine*;
   There's some are fou o' *brandy*;
And mony jobs that day begin,
   May end in *Houghmagandie*
     Some ither day.

(i.e. their hearts of
stone are by night time
as soft as any flesh)
(fou—*full*)

Houghmagandie is one of those indelicate words which are not always translated in glossaries.

The market in communion tokens flourished at least up to 1914; yet about 30 years ago they could hardly be given away. They have now partly come into their own again—an example of how fashion changes in collecting antiques.

HONOURS AND DECORATIONS

The Honours of Scotland
How they survived wars and neglect

Among the most precious objects in the nation's heritage are the Regalia: the Crown, Sceptre, and Sword of State. They are traditionally called the Honours of Scotland. The stories of their survival through times of civil war, their disappearance for more than a century, and their rediscovery are almost without parallel.

The Crown is of unknown age but it is older than any other British crown, for the English crowns were melted for the sake of their gold, or sold, by Oliver Cromwell. Part of the Scottish crown may date from the reign of Robert the Bruce (1306–1329) and it was altered and remodelled in 1540. This was done on the orders of James V and the work was carried out by an Edinburgh goldsmith, John Mosman.

The four arches that go over the top are probably the oldest part and from an older crown. They are of gold and red enamel. The lower part is a circle of gold about eight inches (20.32 cm) across and about an inch and a half (3.8 cm) deep. Round the upper rim of the circle are ten fleurs de lys and ten 'crosses fleury' (crosses in flowers or foliage). On the circle are diamonds, carbuncles, jacinths, amethysts, white topazes and rock crystals. Between the stones are pearls, many of them from Scottish rivers (see page 37). On top of the arches is a globe of gold, the emblem of sovereign authority and majesty, which may have been made in France; it is enamelled in blue and has gilded stars. On top of the globe is a cross with black enamel, pearls, and an amethyst. The cross, too, is probably French. The gold of the Crown was almost certainly mined in Scotland, probably at Crawford Muir.

The Sceptre was given by Pope Alexander VI to James IV in 1494 but James V had it remodelled. The head has three small figures: St Andrew, St James, and the Virgin and Child. On top of these figures is a globe of rock crystal.

The Sword of State was given by Pope Julius II to James IV in 1507. With its sword belt and a consecrated hat it was handed over by the Papal legate and the Abbot of Dunfermline. This was done, with great ceremony, in the Church of Holyrood, Edinburgh. The blade of the sword is 3 feet 3 inches (99 cm) long; the handle and pommel, of gilded silver, are ornamented with oak leaves (the emblem of Julius II); and the transverse guard is in the form of two dolphins. The scabbard, of wood, is covered with crimson silk velvet and has ornaments of gilded silver and enamelled plates.

Civil war, rebellion, religious strife, the accession of children to the throne, and the aggression of England were perpetual themes in the nation's history; yet the regalia survived. A time of great danger was when Cromwell's forces were triumphing against the Covenanting party in 1651. Parliament ordered the Honours of Scotland to be taken to Dunottar Castle, Kincardineshire, which was soon besieged. The garrison was of only 43 men. Inevitably the castle would fall.

The Regalia. On the left, the Sword of State and its scabbard, presented by Pope Julius II to James IV. At the back, the Crown. On the far right, the Lord Treasurer's mace of gilded silver surmounted by a globe of rock crystal. Second from the right, the Sceptre, presented by Pope Alexander VI to James IV and later remodelled. In the centre, a collar of the Order of the Garter, jewelled badges of the Order of the Garter and the Order of the Thistle, and a ruby ring. (The last three are thought to have been taken by James VII and II when he fled the country; they were bequeathed by his descendant Henry, Cardinal of York, to George III.) In front, the Belt of the Sword of State.

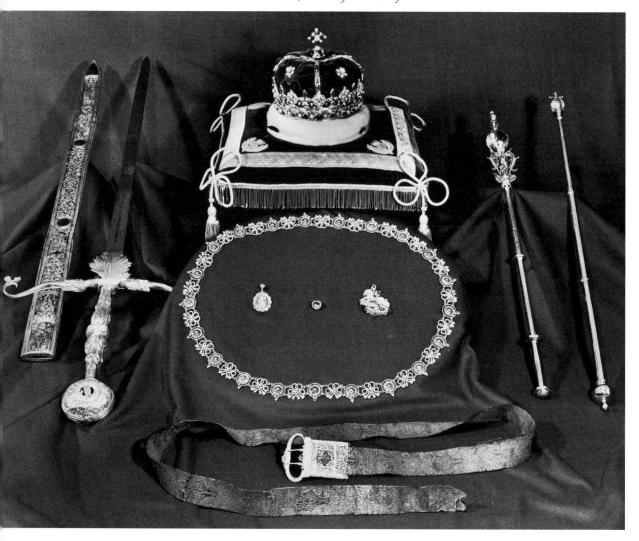

The commander of the castle, George Ogilvie of Barras, was perplexed. His wife and Mrs Christian Granger, the wife of a minister who lived near by, devised a plan. Mrs Granger's servant girl often went to the cliff near the castle, pretending to gather dulse (an edible seaweed) and tangles (other plants). Troops besieging the castle became used to seeing her. At last she was given the Regalia, carried them away 'hid under dulse and coverings', and gave them to Mr and Mrs Granger.

It is said that the treasures were first hidden at the bottom of the bed in the manse. James Granger later told what he did in his church:

For the croun and sceptre I raised the pavement stone just before the pulpit, in the night tyme, and digged under it ane hole, and put them in there, and filled up the hole, and lay doun the stone just as it was before, and removed the mould that remained, that none would have discerned the stone to have been raised at all. The sword again, at the west end of the church, among some common saits that stand there, I digged down in the ground betwixt the twa foremost of these saits, and laid it doun within the case of it, and covered it up, as that removing the superfluous mould it could not be discerned by anybody; for if it shall please God to call me to my death, before they be called for, [you] . . . will find them in that place.

When Dunottar capitulated, the terms included the surrender of the crown, sceptre, and other 'ensigns of Regallitie' and the besiegers were furious to find their quarry had vanished. Ogilvie was heavily fined for breaching the terms of capitulation and he and his wife were imprisoned with rigour in the hope of extracting information from them. Mrs Ogilvie died from the effects of the ill-treatment. She adjured her husband, in her last words, never to reveal the secret.

Until the Restoration of the monarchy nine years later the Regalia were kept safely. Rewards were given to those who had helped in the rescue. Sir John Keith, son of the Earl Marischall, was made Earl of Kintore and Knight Marischall with a salary of £400 a year. Ogilvie was made a baronet and Mrs Granger was given 2000 merks. The next important event was the Act of Union of 1707, which included the provision that 'the Crown, Scepter, and Sword of State . . . continue to be keeped as they are in that part of the United Kingdome now called Scotland, and that they shall so remain in all tyme coming, notwithstanding the Union'.

They were locked up in an oak chest in the Crown Room of Edinburgh Castle on 26 March 1707 and vanished from public sight. Suspicions were later aroused that the Treaty had been broken and that the Regalia had been spirited away to England. Sir Walter Scott and others strongly urged that a search should be carried out in the mysterious locked room of Edinburgh Castle. Scott said in a private letter: 'Our fat friend [the Prince Regent, later George IV] . . . has granted a Commission . . . to the institute a search after the Regalia of Scotland'. The discovery was made on 4 February 1818 and Scott wrote the next day: 'The extreme solemnity of opening sealed doors of oak and iron, and finally breaking open a chest which had been shut . . . about a hundred and eleven years . . . I can hardly describe to you, and it would be very difficult to describe the intense eagerness with which we watched the rising of the lid of the chest, and the progress of the workmen in breaking it open, which was neither an easy nor a speedy task. It sounded very hollow when they worked on it with their tools,' and Scott began to fear that the box would prove to be empty.

The discovery affected Scott deeply. Scott's biographer and son-in-law, J G Lockhart, wrote: 'In the society of Edinburgh at the time, even in the highest Tory circles, it did not seem to awaken much even of curiosity—to say nothing of any deeper feeling. There was, however, a great excitement among the common people of the town, and a still greater among the peasantry, not only in the neighbourhood, but all over Scotland'. The Regalia are now on show in Edinburgh Castle.

The Order of the Thistle

. . . and its rare, costly insignia

Orders and decorations seem to appeal to every sort of society. Even Soviet Russia has, for example, the Order of Lenin. Many have been abolished: the Russian Order of St Vladimir, the Chinese Order of the Golden Cock, the Polish Order of the White Eagle, and dozens of others. But more are being founded as new nations appear on the map of the world: the Liberian Order of African Redemption and the Kenyan Order of the Burning Spear.

Some people collect the insignia as eagerly as the original recipients may have sought the honours. Collectors often specialise in a country or groups of countries, or in a period, or in the higher classes of awards only. Gleaming gold and silver, brilliant enamels, and glittering jewels are not as important as who the owner was and what he did. (Orders are not inscribed with names; British war medals almost always are.) A group of decorations awarded to a known person will be worth several times more than the individual pieces without any known history.

James VII and II decided in 1687 to set up an Order in Scotland that would be comparable with the Garter in the neighbouring kingdom. It was claimed at the time that the Order of the Thistle was a revival of one allegedly founded by a King of Scotland in 787. The basis for the idea was that portraits of Kings of Scotland had medals of St Andrew on gold chains hung round their necks, and St Andrew was the patron of the Thistle as St George was of the Garter.

The first Knights of the Thistle were mainly supporters of James and when he was overthrown in 1688 the Order suffered an eclipse; but it was revived by Queen Anne in 1703. It is probably the most exclusive in Europe: the maximum number of knights was 12 (after the 12 Apostles) until in 1827 the number was fixed at 16. Nowadays the honour is conferred more for deeds than for ancestors.

Insignia of the Thistle are: a *gold collar*, made up of 16 thistles interlaced with sprigs of rue and decorated with coloured enamels. Thistles and rue symbolise the Picts and Scots. From the collar hangs the 'jewel' or collar badge. It has a figure in gold of St Andrew carrying his cross in white enamel and surrounded by golden rays. The *breast star* is in the shape of a St Andrew's Cross; in the centre is a green thistle surrounded by the Order's motto: *Nemo me impune lacessit* (No one

*Insignia of the Order of the Thistle: collar, collar
badge, breast star, and sash badge.*

provokes me with impunity). This item is worn on the left breast. A *sash badge* and a *sash* of rich dark green silk. A knight also wears a *mantle* of green velvet tied with tasselled cords in green and gold. On the left is an embroidered star of the Order.

The insignia are very rare and costly. A new Knight is issued with his insignia by the Central Chancery of the Orders of Knighthood in London and when he dies the insignia must be handed back. Some Knights have their own insignia made privately. From time to time the official issues do slip through the net, are kept by the family, and may appear on the market. A few pieces date from the eighteenth and early nineteenth centuries and are fine examples of Scottish craftsmanship. Among them is a badge of the Order kept with the Scottish Regalia in Edinburgh Castle. The chapel of the Order is in St Giles Cathedral, Edinburgh.

War Medals

History and heroism

Collecting war medals has all the usual fascinations of a hobby but has a bonus. One can relive great battles and great acts of heroism and follow the course of history—and especially the British Empire's victories and defeats. Specialisation is best, and the histories of the Scottish regiments give a great opportunity. (The War Office used to warn its selection boards that candidates' claims to Scottish connections should be examined carefully, because everyone seemed to want to join a Scottish regiment.)

Distress in the Highlands in the eighteenth century, because of the '45 and the harshness of the land, gave the Government a chance to recruit men. No fewer than 20 regiments were raised from the Highlands between 1759 and 1793; loyalty to the chiefs played a big part.

The first British campaign medals were issued after Cromwell's army defeated General Lesley's Scottish troops at Dunbar in 1650. The Scots were trying to put Charles II on the throne. The medal, given to all the officers and men who saw service in Scotland, has on one side Cromwell in armour and, in the background, a view of the battle. The inscription says:

WORD AT		SEPTEM
DUNBAR	THE LORD OF HOSTS	Y.3. 1650

The other side shows the House of Commons in session.

The first medal issued to all soldiers taking part in a campaign was the Waterloo medal of 1815. From these first regular issues onwards the name of the recipient was inscribed on the rim, except during the Second World War. This enables the collector to track down the recipient, the engagement, and the campaign, through the Army and Navy Lists, regimental histories, newspapers, and other records. Medals of other countries are not generally inscribed with the name of the recipients.

Names have sometimes been altered: if a medal was lost the man would buy another and have his name put on it. Such a change is quite innocent, but sometimes alterations have been done to put up the value and an expert eye is needed to tell when this has happened. Sometimes, too, false bars are put on the ribbon.

Condition is not as important as it is with coins, for a certain amount of wear is to be expected and indeed shows that the owner put his medals on and polished them. Far more important the story behind them. A specimen from the Crimea, for example, is especially interesting if the man took part in the charge of the Six Hundred.

The story of the Black Watch* can be taken as just one example of the rich lore of service and heroism of the regiments. Its origin was in some independent companies raised in 1725 to protect the population, stop cattle raiders, and guard against Jacobites who might land from the Continent. They were formed into a regiment, the 43rd of Foot, in 1739, and later became the 42nd. The first of its many battles was in 1745 at Fontenoy against the French and their allies. On the morning of the battle the commanding officer saw the regimental minister, Adam Ferguson, in the ranks with a drawn broadsword. He was told to return to his usual duties or he would lose his commission. He replied: 'Damn my commission' and went on to fight. He later became Professor of Moral Philosophy at Edinburgh University.

The regiment distinguished itself so much at the Battle of Ticonderoga (1758) against the French in North America that it was awarded the title 'Royal'. This battle was a bloody repulse for the men who tried to take a position defended by a morass and a high breastwork. Another desperate engagement was at Quatre Bras (1815), a prelude to the Battle of Waterloo. French cavalry got into the middle of a square formed by the 42nd but the French were all shot or bayoneted. The shattered regiment shortly formed another square with the 44th; French cavalry, infantry, and artillery took a heavy toll. Further distinguished service was in the Crimea, in India during the mutiny, in the Gold Coast against the Ashanti, and in South Africa during the Boer War. The old name of the Black Watch (its origin is obscure) was restored in 1861. All these campaigns and battles are a portrayal in miniature of the nation's history; and can be traced in the medals awarded to the regiment. The same applies to the other regiments.

---

*The regiment had had the honour of appearing in literature: a poem by Thomas Hood.

> Ben Battle was a soldier bold,
>   And used to war's alarms;
> But a cannon-ball took off his legs,
>   So he laid down his arms.
>
> Now as they bore him from the field,
>   Said he, 'Let others shoot,
> For here I leave my second leg,
>   And the Forty-second Foot!'

Commemorative Medals

Propaganda; and events great and small

'I promise by the help of God to abstain from all intoxicating liquors as beverages until I return this medal', says the inscription on a Victorian medal issued by the Edinburgh Industrial Brigade Total Abstinence Association. On the other side is a fountain and: 'Whosoever drinketh of the water that I shall give him shall never thirst. John iv 14'. Another, issued in 1689, celebrates the expulsion of James II and VII. It shows the King with his crown and sceptre falling from his grasp as lightning flashes towards him; and an orange tree (for William of Orange, his successor) entwined with roses and thistles. With the King in his flight is his infant son carrying a windmill (rumour said the child's father was not James but a miller). Snakes of discord accompany their flight.

Medals have been issued as propaganda; or to mark notable events such as the Battle of Culloden and the visit of George IV to Edinburgh in 1822; or to honour achievement in sport, agriculture, or learning. They are often of great historic interest and artistic merit but have been comparatively neglected. They are often linked in people's minds with coins, yet they are different in several ways. Coins have to circulate and so are in low relief and usually show signs of wear. Medals are to be cherished and are often in larger size and in high relief with little signs of wear. Coins are issued by Governments and monarchs. Medals are generally issued by private institutions for their own purposes or by individuals and firms for their own profit.

Collecting medals does have its problems. Plenty of basic handbooks have been written but no comprehensive catalogue: the numbers issued over the centuries have been so vast that the task is almost impossible. A knowledge of Latin is a help because the inscriptions are often in Latin—and abbreviated at that. Part of the interest is doing research into the historical background. A late eighteenth-century piece has a portrait of Admiral Duncan, who was from Perthshire. The reverse side has a sailor nailing a flag to a masthead and the inscriptions: 'October 11, 1797, with 24 ships and 1198 guns defeated the Dutch fleet of 25 ships and 1259 guns: 9 ships and 592 guns taken'; and 'Heroic courage protects the British flag'. A sailor nailed the flag to a mast during the action—the Battle of Camperdown— to stop the flag being struck or brought down.

An example of political medals is one with the legend: 'Renfrewshire Political Union. Instituted 3rd Decr 1830. To obtain a radical reform of our national abuses'. On the reverse are a dove of peace, a cap of liberty, the sword and

Medal awarded to Sir Colin Campbell (1776–1847), who served with great distinction in India and against Napoleon. This medal is the Peninsular Gold Cross with six clasps. Campbell ran away from Perth Academy when he was sixteen and went to sea. He became a soldier and rose to be a general. He was present at Waterloo and was a close friend of Wellington.

This medal was sold, along with several other awards and decorations, at Christie's in 1974. It was sent in the group by a direct descendant, and fetched £12,000. A group of medals and decorations given to a notable personage will make more than individual items with no known history.

balance of Justice, the cornucopia of plenty, the thistle, rose, and shamrock, and: 'Reform Bills the means of extending the elective franchise and of obtaining a just, cheap, and peaceful government'.

Politics and especially the monarchy were favourite themes until the beginning of the Victorian era. Many Jacobite medals were produced, some of them with the same decoration as Jacobite glasses (see page 107). One shows a bust of the Young Pretender and the legend 'Carolus Walliae Princeps, 1745'. (Charles, Prince of Wales.) On the reverse is Britannia resting on her spear and shield and standing near a globe, on the shore. She watches the approach of a fleet. This was probably made when Charles was planning his invasion. Britannia represents the country looking forward with hope to his arrival.

Culloden inspired more medals than any other event in Scottish history. They vary in workmanship from excellent to crude. One of the more crude shows the Duke of Cumberland galloping on a horse with drawn sword; on the reverse is the Young Pretender trying to reach a crown on a pillar; the Duke is pulling him back and running him through with a sword. The misspelled but satirical legend is: 'Come back again Pretenter.'

The universities, colleges, and schools gave medals to clever students although these tend to be for medicine, divinity, and such traditional subjects. Golf, curling, and other sporting clubs gave awards. The long-established firm of Alexander Kirkwood in Edinburgh has made many for all sorts of occasions and its name can be detected in small lettering.

Pieces made before the end of the eighteenth century tend to be scarce and expensive; in the nineteenth century techniques of production improved and many more medals were issued. Spurious examples are found: for example, by casts taken from original specimens. But this field is much less dangerous than others.

The recent boom in coin collecting has affected medals and since the mid-1960s a flood of new issues has poured forth. The utmost skills of the marketing men are used to promote them and the most diverse occasions are commemorated: reproductions of Old Master paintings, the history of the car, wildlife, royalty (even the royal corgis). They have been promoted as investments but some buyers have been cruelly disappointed—their 'investments' have from time to time turned out to be worth little more than the scrap value of the metal. Much depends on the quality of the design and of the workmanship and on the interest of the subject. Moreover, the size of the 'edition'—the number of copies made— affects the value as an investment. The more copies that are made, the less likely in general is the value to go up. Some editions are advertised as 'limited' but they

Medal in gold to commemorate the return of Charles I to London from his coronation at Scone in 1651. The reverse shows a view of London with old St Paul's and London Bridge. It is by a noted designer and craftsman of coins and medals, Nicholas Briot, and was worth about £2600 in 1976.

Medal in gold to commemorate the coronation of Charles II at Scone in 1651. His coronation in London was not until after the Restoration in 1660. The lion rampant holds a thistle. Worth about £2100 in 1976.

may be limited to as many as 5000, which is fairly high; or the limit may be the number applied for by a certain date.

Medals perhaps originated in ancient Greece. For example a large specimen made in Syracuse, the Greek colony in Sicily, appears to have been a prize for an athlete. Italian princes of the fifteenth and sixteenth centuries, seeking to be patrons of art and to magnify their own importance at the same time, commissioned medals from distinguished artists such as Pisanello. The collector, faced with an enormous choice, has to specialise and Scottish themes are as good as any. Someone who is a specialist can pick up bargains.

SNUFF AND BOXES

Tobacconists' Figures

The Highlander—a sign of good snuff

When most people could not read or write the shopkeepers and tradesmen put painted wooden symbols or painted boards outside their premises. A goldsmith and jeweller might have a golden cup, a wool merchant some bales of wool, a pawnbroker three brass balls, and so on. Sellers of snuff for years used figures of Highlanders because the Scots were famous for their snuff.

The first signs for tobacconists were of Princess Pocahontas, an Indian who came to Britain in 1616 with her husband Captain John Rolfe and caused a sensation. Figures of her were superseded by blackamoors or black boys with crowns and skirts of tobacco leaves. Others were Turks, sailors, Indian princes, and—especially in the United States—American Indians.

The Highlanders began in 1720 when David Wishart, who came from Edinburgh, put up a six-foot high carved Highlander outside his shop in central London. It wore doublet and trews and had a claymore and targe.

Compton Mackenzie wrote in his book *Sublime Tobacco*: 'There was no snuff-mull in his hand, and he stood there . . . not to advertise David Wishart's wares but to let loyal gentlemen know that at the back of the shop they might discuss safely the prospect of the King's coming into his own again.' The King was James VIII, the Old Pretender.

Figures of Highlanders came to be an accepted sign of a place where Jacobites met. Compton Mackenzie also wrote: 'With that superlative capacity for extracting romance out of commerce and even more remarkably, commerce out of romance, which has been the secret of Scottish vitality, the Scottish tobacco dealers in London recognised the attraction of the Highlander outside Wishart's shop . . . presently he was given the kilt instead of trews and instead of a targe and claymore a snuff-mull in his hand to become the recognised sign of the tobacconist who kept the best snuff.'

The rising of '45 and the forbidding of Highland dress (see page 8) brought these figures into trouble. A mock petition was circulated:

We hear that the dapper Wooden Highlanders who so heroically guard the doors of snuff shops intend to petition the Legislature in order that they may be excused from complying with the Act of Parliament with respect to the change of dress, alleging that they have ever been faithful subjects of His Majesty, having constantly supplied his Guards with a pinch out of their mulls when they marched by ; and, so far from engaging

From left to right:

A bearded Highlander smoking a pipe and holding a pinch of snuff and a mull. 32½ inches high (82.5 cm) and made about 1780. Sold by Christie's in 1975 for £420.

A Highland soldier with red jacket and holding a pinch of snuff and a mull. 37 inches (94 cm) high and made about 1780. Sold by Christie's in 1975 for £360.

A Highland soldier with plumed bonnet and red jacket and holding a pinch of snuff and mull. 31 inches (79 cm) high and made about 1780. Sold by Christie's in 1975 for £300.

in any rebellion, that they have never entertained a rebellious thought: Whence they humbly hope that they shall not be put to the expence of buying new clothes.

It seems that the figures did fall out of popularity—after all, the Government and many sections of society had been severely jolted by the '45. But times changed, the ban on Highland dress was ended, and the figures reappeared all over the country, and in Scotland especially. Many of the surviving ones are in the uniforms of officers of the Peninsular War period when Scottish regiments distinguished themselves. Large figures stood at the door of the shop and smaller ones over the door or window or on the counter. They were brightly painted to catch the eye and to protect the wood. They seem to have gone out of general use in about 1845.

Snuff Mulls

Containers of ivory, wood, or horn

Snuff and snuff-taking were called sneesh and sneeshing. Distinctive sorts of snuff containers were made, and they were called mulls.

The habit seems to have gripped the Scots before the English. A kirk decree as early as 1641 said that 'every one that takes snuff in tyme of Divine service, shall pay 6/8 pence, and give ane public confession for their fault'. The rest of the country took up the habit later, and especially in the eighteenth century.

Some very fancy varieties of snuff were invented on the Continent and in England: they were perfumed with, for example, orange, violet, lily of the valley, civet (from a cat-like tropical animal), musk (from a Himalayan deer), cedar, and wine. Along with these additives went harmful adulterations. But the Scots did not take to fripperies and their snuff, made only from stalks of tobacco, was renowned for purity.

'Mull' is a curious word. It seems likely that the original mulls were containers with graters, grinders, or mills to powder the tobacco; but when the tobacco could be bought ready ground the term mull may have been given to the receptacle. 'Mill' is pronounced 'mull' in broad Scots.

Almost any small container will do for snuff, but vase-shaped mulls appeared some time around 1680. Some of them were made in the same way as barrels and quaichs (for quaichs, see page 67). Staves of ebony and ivory were fitted together and bound at the top and bottom with bands of metal, usually silver. Vase-shaped mulls of wood, ivory, or horn were made with a lathe. Mulls of amber, mother-of-pearl, tortoiseshell, jasper, rubies, diamonds, enamel, and such-like costly materials may be from the Continent.

Jacobite themes are sometimes found in the decoration. The original owners sometimes had their initials and a date engraved on the metal mounts. 'His' and 'Hers' pairs of these mulls are known; the man's is slightly bigger than the woman's. Hinges are often large and bold and vaguely resemble the open wings of a butterfly—this form is distinctively Scottish. Mulls of this shape went out of fashion in the mid-eighteenth century and curly-ended horn mulls came in. Such a

A snuff mull mounted in silver by William Jameson of Aberdeen in about 1810. It is inscribed around the rim: 'To the London Society of the Sons of the Clergy of the Established Church of Scotland from Skene Oglivy, DD, Minister of Aberdeen, first charge'. The lid has a polished pebble or semi-precious stone and the implements were for the ceremony of taking the snuff.

mull in the horn's original shape would not do because the pointed end would poke a hole in the pocket. The end was therefore curled by heating and bending it. Mounts of silver and cairngorms or other stones added to the charm. Other mounts are of brass, pewter, or iron.

Far bigger mulls were made from about 1770 for standing on tables and were used by regimental messes, clubs, burgh councils, trade corporations, and so forth as well as in private houses. These mulls are of a longer section of the animal's horns, or even an entire ram's head preserved by a taxidermist. The ram's head had a receptacle on top for holding the snuff. The receptacle and the ends of the horns are usually adorned with cairngorms. (For cairngorms, see page 36.)

Silver bands or shields were attached to these mulls and inscribed with the names of the organisation's officials. Tiny implements were attached by chains: a mallet for dislodging snuff which might get stuck on the side of the mull, a spike to break it up if it got lumpy, a rake to smooth the surface, a spoon for placing it on the hand, a hare's foot for sweeping up stray grains. Table mulls tended to be so big that they were made with little wheels so that they could easily be circulated round the table.

The habit has had its ups and downs. Queen Elizabeth condemned it in 1584. The Tsar Michael decreed in 1634 that a person found guilty for the second time of taking snuff would have his nose cut off. Pope Urban VIII issued a Bill in 1635 excommunicating anyone who took snuff in church; it was 'an abomination in the sight of God that the clergy take snuff at ecclesiastical councils'. The city of Bern included in the Ten Commandments a prohibition of tobacco. But in the eighteenth century the manner of taking snuff became an important social grace with its own etiquette. Enormous sums were lavished on the boxes in France during the eighteenth century and the finest specimens are masterpieces of the jeweller's and goldsmith's art. Lord Petersham (1780–1851) had a special room in his house for keeping his supplies and filling his boxes; when he died he had 2000 lb (907 kg). But snuffing was in decline from the 1830s onwards, and by 1850 was out of fashion. A book on etiquette said in 1834: 'As snuff taking is merely an idle, dirty habit, practised by stupid people in the unavailing endeavour to clear their stupid intellect, and is not a custom particularly offensive to their neighbours, it may be to each individual taste as to whether it be continued or not. An "Elegant" cannot take *much* snuff without decidedly "losing caste" '.

A 'table compendium' for snuff, made by James Myres of Edinburgh in 1891. The container on top is of silver ornamented with thistles and scrolling foliage and inset with an imitation semi-precious stone. The implements on chains are rabbit's foot, probe, scoop, rake, and ivory hammer. The height is 13½ inches (34.3 cm). This was sold by Sotheby's in 1972 for £290.

The Secret Hinge

Boxes for snuff and tea

Snuff is an awkward substance. It is so fine that it leaks easily from containers. It stains clothes. It is unpleasant when it flies about in the air. Moreover, wooden snuff boxes are not the ideal containers. Wood takes in moisture from the air in humid conditions and gives out moisture in dry conditions. This means that it tends to swell and shrink. Lids of ordinary wooden snuff boxes are thus liable to come loose and let the snuff get out.

Many British snuff boxes in the eighteenth century were of wood, were circular, and had detachable lipped lids. A great improvement was devised and made: a type of hinge which fitted perfectly and could be produced in large numbers. 'Knuckles' or joints were cut on the box and on the lid. Holes were drilled through them and a pin of brass threaded through the holes to hold the lid and box together. The holes at the ends were stopped up with wood. The person who mechanised the manufacture of these hinges was a legless, bed-ridden genius— James Sandy of Alyth, Perthshire. The *Dundee Advertiser* wrote in 1819, soon after his death:

At twelve years of age, he had the misfortune to injure one of his legs by a fall from a tree; and having the additional misfortune to apply to a quack-doctor, he entirely lost the use of it, after a confinement of some years. At this period, he set about making a violin; in which he succeeded wonderfully well considering that his only tools were a gouge and a knife. He persevered in this employment for some time; and having procured better tools, he became more perfect in his employment, and finished his violins in a very neat style. He next made flutes, clarionets, bagpipes, fishing-rods, etc. in the same superior manner; every part of the work being performed by himself. He also amused himself in taming various kinds of birds, which gave rise to a report that he hatched geese by the heat of his body. This is one of those vague reports which it behoves the candid historian to correct: for the fact is simply this,—that a gosling, which had been hatched by a hen, having been left an *orphan* at a very tender age, James took compassion on it, and reared it till it became a *perfect goose*; and it afterwards lived with him for eight or nine years, always evincing the greatest attachment to its kind protector.

One would have thought that a man who had been confined to one spot for about five years, ran very little risk of more accident to his limbs. But it happened, that one winter, when the ice on the Burn of Alyth broke up, it gorged at the Bridge; and caused the water to rise so very high as to inundate the lower part of the house where sat the unfortunate James. As he was totally unable to move, his mother endeavoured to drag him up stairs, beyond the reach of the flood; and in the attempt, unluckily broke the sound leg. Poor James was thus rendered a complete cripple; and, during the rest of his life, he sat constantly during the day on what served him for a bed at night. Now applying himself wholly to mechanics, he made several eight-day clocks; one of which played twelve tunes on bells. He afterwards studied optics; and made several telescopes both plain and reflecting; casting and turning the brasswork, making and polishing the speculums, grinding the glasses, and wholly finished them, without any assistance; except occasionally that of a person to turn his lathe, when the work was too heavy for his hands.

He made artificial teeth; and a weaver in the neighbourhood having lost his arm by a threshing-mill, James made an artificial one, jointed so that the man could continue to work at his trade. For this he received a reward of ten guineas from the Trustees for the Encouragement of Arts and Manufactures. He excelled in making wooden snuff boxes, such as are made at Laurencekirk; painted and varnished them himself; constructed a most ingenious machine for cutting their hinges; made circular saws, and every other kind of tool necessary for his various occupations. He knew a little music; and could play on the violin, flute and clarionet. He made several electrical machines; was an engraver, carver, and gilder, and was armourer to the Volunteers while they continued embodied. In short, there was no piece of mechanism, however ingenious, but James Sandy could copy; and that very often in a manner superior to the original. He had a manly, expressive

Vase-shaped snuff mulls, and sold by Sotheby's in 1975—left to right:

Silver mull of about 1750, richly decorated with scrolls, birds, scales, fishes, and matting, £105.

Lignum vitae and ivory in alternating staves, about 1760, £70. Lignum vitae is a hard, heavy, and dark wood from the West Indies and tropical America.

Ivory, about 1760, £80.

Lignum vitae with bands of ivory round the base and rim, about 1760, £50.

countenance, and was extremely civil and courteous to his visitors, among whom he could reckon most people of rank or fortune in his neighbourhood, and frequently strangers from a distance, attracted by curiosity to see so extraordinary a genius. His townspeople often intruded upon him to while away a leisure hour. The conversation was apt to get dry. Whisky was sent for to enliven it; and James sometimes partook of it to a greater extent than was good for him.

Commercial manufacture of boxes with integral wooden hinges was done by Charles Stiven of Laurencekirk, Kincardineshire, which is only about 20 miles from Alyth. The boxes were prettily decorated by hand. Other boxes such as tea caddies were made as snuff-taking became less fashionable.

Stiven's sponsor was a wealthy eccentric, Francis Garden, Lord Gardenstone,

who was described as 'an acute and able lawyer, of great natural eloquence and
with much wit and humour'. He was wealthy and well read. He began in 1765 to
build a new village at Laurencekirk, brought in new manufactures, and built a
library and museum.

Many stories were told about him; for example in William Hone's *Year Book*:

Lord Gardenstone . . . who died in 1793, also a lord of session and author of several
literary works, had strange eccentric fancies, in his mode of living; he seemed to indulge
these chiefly with a view to his health, which was always that of a valetudinarian. He had a
predilection for pigs. A young one took a particular fancy for his Lordship, and followed
him wherever he went like a dog, reposing in the same bed. When it attained the years and
size of swinehood, this was inconvenient. However, his Lordship, unwilling to part with
his friend, continued to let it sleep in his bed room, and, when he undressed, laid his
clothes upon the floor, as a bed to it. He said that he liked the pig, for it kept his clothes
warm till the morning.

The secret of how to make the hinge was valuable but Laurencekirk lost it and
rival firms arose in Ayrshire. The details of how this happened are not clear, for
several different accounts have been given of it; but the main points are known.

Sir Alexander Boswell, son of James the biographer of Dr Johnson, had guests
staying at his home, Auchinleck House, near Old Cumnock, Ayrshire, at some
time around 1806 or 1807. Sir James or one of his guests broke the hinge of his
Laurencekirk snuffbox and sent it for mending to a local watchmaker and
gunsmith, named Wyllie. He had an employee called William, John, or George
Crawford who tried to do the repair. Solder, however, ran into the hinge. Melting
the solder out would have destroyed the box, so Crawford made an instrument
to cut the solder away. This was a big step towards unlocking the secret of making
the hinge. Wyllie and Crawford devised jigs and other tools to do the job and
seem to have established a flourishing business.

Others too found out the secret. Soon the hinged boxes were being made in the
villages of Old Cumnock, New Cumnock, Mauchline, and other places. The rival
makers undercut each others' prices and went in for a wider range of products.
The trade reached the peak of its prosperity in the 1820s.

The early boxes were decorated with painted pictures or pen-and-ink work.
Themes include shooting, fishing, and hunting; picturesque views; Scottish
dancing; and pastoral scenes. This was expensive to do. Cheaper wares were
needed for the business to survive. From about 1820 the decoration was done in
chequer and tartan patterns which were less artistic but more mechanical. The
next phase was the rise of the goods now called Mauchline ware.

Mauchline Ware

Inexpensive wooden souvenirs

The Victorians had a passion for souvenirs of the places they visited on holiday.
They also had a romantic attachment to Scotland which was encouraged by the
example of Victoria and Albert. Demand for Scottish souvenirs was met partly by

Mauchline ware made in the late nineteenth century with views of English seaside resorts including Brighton, Bournemouth, and Skegness; all the objects are in sycamore. They are (from left): *money box, pin box, needle case, holder for ball of wool, spectacle case, bottle case, tape measure in holder shaped like a bell, and a bottle case.*

an industry that flourished in Mauchline, Ayrshire, and other small towns and villages. This was in the making of Mauchline ware, useful small objects in wood. Mauchline ware is decorated with views of notable buildings, pretty landscapes, holiday resorts, famous people, and tartans. A brisk export trade was built up and souvenirs were also made for places in England and Wales, the Continent, Australia, India and the United States.

The range of objects is enormous: boxes of all sorts, egg cups, letter racks, paper knives, spectacle cases, book covers, photograph frames, brushes, and many more. Some of them reflect customs and needs that are almost forgotten: cases for visiting cards, snuff boxes, glove stretchers, parasol handles, toothpick holders, stands for holding pocket watches at night. Collectors tend at first to buy freely and later to concentrate on getting a variety of different pieces. The wood used was mostly sycamore, which grows to perfection in Scotland. It is fairly free of knots, has a close texture, takes a smooth finish, and does not warp if it has been properly seasoned. It is creamy white when first cut but the makers varnished it and that gave it a more yellow tint.

Scottish views are the most frequently found, and especially of the Burns country. Some of the other places are Edinburgh, the Border Abbeys, Stirling, Dunkeld, dozens of stately homes, and even quite small villages. Some of the souvenirs were of wood from famous or romantic spots such as Flodden Field, Birnham Wood, and the Banks of Doon; but some of these sales angles may have been fraudulent. It is improbable that the Banks of Doon had enough trees to supply all the timber needed for a huge output of pieces.

The English views include St Paul's Cathedral, colleges in Oxford, the Shakespeare country, the pier at Eastbourne, and the Royal Observatory at Greenwich. A tourist going to the Continent might bring back Mauchline ware with views of Paris, Boulogne, Cannes or Nice—and that same object may appear nowadays in a junk shop or antique shop in this country.

Mauchline ware is comparatively cheap and easy to store because of the small size. But it should not be kept in a centrally heated room. Central heating makes the atmosphere very dry and moisture tends to be sucked out of objects made of wood, leather, ivory, and similar vegetable or animal materials. The result, in wooden objects, can be warping and splitting. Souvenir woodware was originally decorated by hand, with paint or pen and ink. This was costly and the makers turned to more mechanical ways. Demand was high and prices had to be kept down—some of the objects sold for as little as sixpence. Engravings on metal were made of the designs; these were printed on paper and pressed on to the surface of the souvenir. Then the paper was removed and the design was left. This 'transfer' method was the most widely used. Even quicker and cheaper ways were brought in. Photographs were used instead of prints and were stuck on and varnished over.

Tartan souvenirs were made in a similar way—at first painted directly on to the wood and later printed on paper and glued to the surface. The name of the tartan was usually given in gold lettering. It took a lot of skill to fit the patterned paper on to a curved surface such as a parasol handle. Another variation was to stick on ferns gathered from the Isle of Arran. Brown paint was then spattered on the object; the fern was removed; and an outline was left. The final stage was to varnish the whole object. The search for cost-cutting changed this too. Paper was printed with patterns of fern and stuck on; photographs of fern were used too.

One firm dominated the industry: W and A Smith of Mauchline, who also had factories in Birmingham for a while. The Smiths were enterprising, inventive, and persistent in the face of difficulties. They devised processes and machinery and survived all their competitors. They probably made more than half the Mauchline ware and reached the peak of their success in the mid-1860s. But by the end of the century business was in a bad way. The Smiths' success brought competition from the Continent, especially from Germany. Mass-produced souvenirs in other materials cut into the trade. Scottish thread-making firms at one time packaged their products in Mauchline boxes and miniature barrels, to attract custom. This important outlet was lost when thread-making firms amalgamated and competition was not so keen.

Off-the-peg clothing and the spread of sewing machines to many homes transformed the demand for thread and the way it was packaged. A severe blow came in 1933 when the Smiths' premises in Mauchline were destroyed by fire; the firm closed down when the Second World War broke out.

A curious thing has happened since the heyday: the products were formerly called 'Scotch goods', 'clan tartan woodwork' and 'white wood work'. Only in fairly recent times have they been called Mauchline Ware.

STUARTS AND JACOBITES

Stuart Relics

Tragedies of a royal line

The misfortunes of the House of Stuart have aroused sympathy and loyalty: the imprisonment and execution of Mary Queen of Scots, the execution of Charles I, the deposition of James VII and II, the struggles of the Jacobite cause. Some people hold that the rightful King of Britain is the head of the House of Wittelsbach, the former royal house of Bavaria and in theory the heir of the Stuarts' claims.

Mary Queen of Scots fled from her rebellious subjects to England and was imprisoned from 1568 to 1587. Her plotting against Queen Elizabeth ended with her execution at Fotheringhay Castle in 1587. The English Government feared that her followers would make a cult of venerating her relics and took steps to prevent that happening. Her clothes, for example, were burned after her execution instead of being the perquisite of the executioner. But locks of her hair have been preserved. She bequeathed her gold rosary and crucifix to the Countess of Arundel and it descended in the family of the Dukes of Norfolk, the premier Roman Catholics of England. The British Museum has a signet ring and the Victoria and Albert Museum has her veil.

Charles I was beheaded in Whitehall on 30 January 1648 (Old Style, or before the calendar was reformed—the new year began in March. The date was 30 January 1649 by present reckoning). It was a cold day and he did not want to shiver, lest the multitude who watched thought he was shivering with fear; so he wore two shirts. Both have been preserved, one at Windsor Castle and the other at Longleat House, Wiltshire. Spectators rushed to dip their handkerchiefs in the royal blood. Reports soon circulated that these relics were effecting miraculous cures. The executioner sold handfuls of blood-spattered sand from the scaffold and pieces of blood-soaked wood. Locks of the king's hair were cut and sold. The prayer book he carried on that day came into the ownership of John Evelyn, the diarist, who wrote in it: 'This is the Booke which Charles the First M.B. [Martyr Beatus, or Blessed Martyr] did use upon the Scaffold xxx Jan. 1648, being the day of his glorious martyrdom.' It was sold in 1825 for £105. The blue silk garment he wore over his shirts was sold in 1898 for £210 and a nail from the scaffold for £6 16s 6d. (£6.82½).

His admirers commemorated his death with innumerable rings, lockets, pendants, medallions, and so forth. A large collection of such things was sold by

Left: a pendant in the shape of a book, $2\frac{1}{2}$ inches (6.4 cm) high and made in the mid seventeenth century. It is of silver and gilded metal. Inside is a portrait in gilded silver of Charles I and a piece of blood-stained cloth. The outside is decorated with a crown, the initials CR, open gold work, and crystals. Sold at Christie's in 1975 for £982. Top right: a gold ring with a miniature of Charles I and set with diamonds and pastes. It was made in about 1650. Rings like this were presented by Queen Henrietta Maria in return for financial support. They were to be redeemed when the Civil War was over. Some were redeemed for the amount of the loan or for an honour. This was sold at Christie's in 1975 for £577.50. Bottom right: a miniature of Charles I, $\frac{1}{2}$ inch (1.8 cm) high, and painted in the eighteenth century. It is set in a gold ring. It was sold at Christie's in 1975 for £184.80.

A linen handkerchief said to have been carried by Charles I at his execution and to have been acquired by Robert Spavin, personal secretary to Cromwell. It has three tassels, and the embroidered initials CR with a crown. A note which accompanied the handkerchief said: 'Not to be washed lest the bloodstains of His late Majesty be removed'. This was sold at Christie's in 1975 for £350.

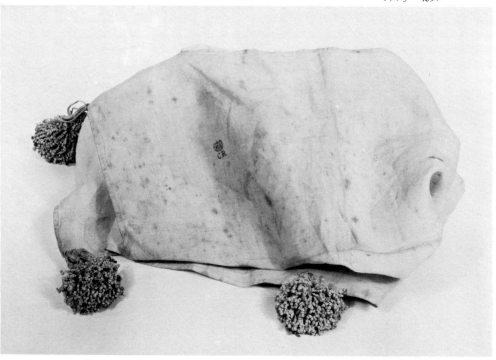

Christie's in 1973 and 1975. A reliquary in the form of a tiny metal book fetched £982. It is of copper, silvered and gilded and with a jewel, crystals and enamels. It contains a portrait of the King and a piece of blood-stained cloth and dates from about 1650. A silver pendant, containing under a glass lid a piece of cloth traditionally held to be a part of Charles I's shroud, was sold for £147. The pendant has large crystals, and the initials CR with a crown, enamelled in colours. A silver snuffbox, made in Dublin about 1830 but containing a lock of hair said to be Charles I's, was sold for £196.35. Sold with the box was a scientific analysis which, according to Christie's, 'although inconclusive does not rule out the possibility that the hair is that of Charles I'. A silk garter of about 1648, 50 inches (127 cm) long, was sold for £126. It has the words GOD BLESS THE KING AND DOWN WITH THE RUMP'. The Rump was the remnant of the Long Parliament and was in existence from 1648 to 1653. Garters of this length could be worn either crossed around the leg or tied with a bow.

Relics of the Young Pretender have survived—such as gifts from him to the people who sheltered him during his flight after the Battle of Culloden. Among these objects are his sporran, dagger, gloves, yellow satin waistcoat, and rings. His travelling 'canteen' was captured at Culloden and given by 'Butcher' Cumberland to an aide de camp for carrying the news of the battle to London. The canteen is a silver container in the shape of a flask seven inches (17.8 cm) high, engraved with the Prince of Wales's feathers (the Young Pretender was regarded as the rightful Prince of Wales because his father was still alive). The canteen was made in Edinburgh in 1740 and held knives, forks, spoons, spice containers, and so on.

Jacobite Glasses

A toast to the King over the Water

The loyalty and hope of the Jacobites were sustained through years of disappointment; and one of the ways this was done was through secret and semi-secret clubs. Sociable drinking gave a chance for tangible expressions of the common cause: glasses engraved with portraits and semi-secret symbols and slogans. Toasts were drunk to the King—but the glasses were sometimes held over a bowl of water, so that the King was really 'the King over the Water', that is the exiled James III or Charles III. (Finger bowls were banned from royal dinner tables until the death of Queen Victoria in 1901, lest a Jacobite toast be drunk 'over the water' in the presence of the non-Jacobite sovereign.)

The symbols on the glasses had to be semi-secret because being a Jacobite was at times risky. Scholars have worked out what most of them mean but doubts still remain. The symbols include: the *rose*, for the Crown of England—the rose being of course the national flower of England. The rose on the glasses has either one or two *buds*, signifying the Old Pretender, the Young Pretender, or both. The *thistle* stands for the Scottish Crown but is much scarcer than the rose. The *oak leaf* is the longed-for restoration of the Stuart house. Charles II hid in the Boscabel Oak after his defeat at the Battle of Worcester. He wore oak leaves when he entered

London in triumph at the Restoration of 1660. A *stricken oak tree* is the unfortunate Stuart house. It may have one or two saplings or two sprouting leaves—the two rightful heirs. A *forget-me-not* is in memory of the Old Pretender who died in 1766. A *daffodil* is also thought to signify mourning for him. A *carnation* may mean the Crown: the indentation of the petals resemble a crown, according to one theory. Or it may stand for Carolus (Charles). Another emblem, the honeysuckle, may stand for Henricus (Henry Cardinal York).

The Old Pretender was nicknamed 'blackbird' by his family because of his dark complexion and this symbol appears. And a *jay* stands for James or Jacobite. The *star* is the guiding aim or principle of the cause. The *compass* is thought to be the emblem of one particular club, perhaps the Cycle Club, and is very rare. A *grub* or grubs appear and have puzzled scholars. Some people hold that the significance is the enemies of the cause, or its traitors, or its decline. Other people hold that the grub has to do with the belief that the soul of a Scotsman who dies abroad returns to his native land by the 'low road', or underground. *Butterflies, moths, caterpillars, bees* and *flies* have not been fully solved. Inscriptions are generally in Latin:

Ab obice major—The great often fall

Audentior ibo—I shall go more boldly

Fiat—May it happen

Hic vir hic est—This, this is the man

Reddas incolumen—May you return safely

Redi, or *redite*, or *redeat*—May he return

Other inscriptions are in English and some rare ones are in shorthand. 'A Halth to I . . . ms' is easy; 'The Faithful Palinurus' is on a glass at Dunvegan Castle, Skye, and refers to the bravery of Flora Macdonald in guiding Charles to safety after Culloden when he was pursued by the Government's troops. Palinurus was Aeneas's pilot. This glass also has inscribed on it the Jacobite version of the national anthem. Such glasses are extremely rare—perhaps 24 or a few more exist—but dangerous fakes were made in the 1930s. They are called Amen glasses because the inscription ends with the word.

Portraits are mostly of the Young Pretender and—very rare—of Flora Macdonald.

Jacobite glasses were in many cases made and decorated in Newcastle upon Tyne, the main centre of glassmaking in Britain. Later examples tend to be of poor quality with crude engraving. Genuine eighteenth-century glasses, originally plain, have been engraved with Jacobite themes in modern times. One way of spotting them is to look at the engraving, which ought to show signs of age.

The opponents of the Jacobite cause had their own commemorative glass, called Williamite because they celebrated William of Orange's coming to the throne. A typical goblet is engraved with a portrait of the King and 'The Glorious and Immortal Memory of King William and his Queen Mary and Perpetual disappointment to the Pope the Pretender and all the Enemies of the Protestant Religion'.

Another has: 'To the glorious pious and immortal memory of the great and good King William who freed us from Pope and Popery, knaves and slavery, brass money and wooden shoes. And he who refuses this toast may be damned, crammed and rammed down the great gun of Athlone.' Most Williamite glasses— perhaps all—seem to have been made in Ireland and to date from the second half of the eighteenth century.

Jacobite clubs that used these glasses seem to have disguised themselves as being merely social and convivial. The oldest was the Gloucestershire Society, which was found in 1657 and which lasted until about 1840; at the end it was for people with antiquarian interests. The Oyster and Parched Pea Club at Preston, Lancashire, lasted from about 1771 until 1841. It was strongly Tory and membership was confined to 12 leading citizens. A barrel of oysters was sent by

Jacobite glass with the symbolic rose and bud; on the other side is a thistle. It is 6½ inches (16.5 cm). Sold at Christie's in 1976 for £66.

Left: an anti-Jacobite glass with a portrait of the Duke of Cumberland, victor of Culloden. Right: *an 'Amen' glass with the Jacobite version of the National Anthem.*

wagon from London to be on the club's table every Monday during the oyster season. The office-bearers included an Oystericus and a Clerk of the Peas. This apparent frivolity may have been to disguise political discussion, for no outsider was admitted to meetings until 1784. The Royal Oak Club was founded in Edinburgh in 1772 and met on the first Monday of the month. A club called the Cycle of the White Rose was founded in North Wales in 1710, survived until the 1820s, and may have continued to meet every year until about 1850. Another club in South Wales called the Sea-Serjeants may have been Jacobite but was so secretive that its politics, if any, are not known.

Affection for the cause survived in the North American colonies. A scheme for making Charles II the King of Virginia was mooted during the Protectorate; and a similar scheme was mooted for Charles III. But the vital documents about this apparently vanished from the Royal Archives some time in the first half of the nineteenth century.

Charles III, or the Young Pretender, died in 1788, his last years marred by disappointment, drink, wanderings, and an unhappy marriage. The heir was his brother Henry Cardinal York, or Henry IX, a wealthy man with incomes from land in Mexico (granted to him by the King of Spain) and from two abbeys in France. But he lost his American income because European wars interrupted traffic by sea; his French income disappeared during the Revolution; invading French troops sacked his home at Frascati, near Rome. He was in dire poverty by 1800 and the British Government gave him £5000 a year. He died in 1807.

THE ARTS

James and William Tassie
Portrait medallions and copies of gems

A craze for a new style swept Britain in the 1760s. This was neo-classicism, an attempt to return to the 'true' classical forms of architecture, art, furniture, silver, and so on. The great exponent was Robert Adam (1728–1792), who became the leading architect of his time. His father, William, was a leading Edinburgh architect and Robert's brothers John, James and William all went into the profession.

The movement was partly inspired by excavations at Pompeii and Herculaneum, buried by an eruption of Vesuvius in AD 79. The excavations, from 1738, were carried out with enthusiasm but not at first with much scientific care. (The ash and lava were dug for treasures as if the site was a mine; the King of Naples thought of the finds as a valuable source of income.)

One of the symptoms of the craze for neo-classicism was the eager collecting of classical, renaissance, and contemporary engraved gems—hardstones such as chalcedony and agate carved with figures and symbols. But classical gems were in short supply and the gap was filled by reproductions. James Tassie, a Scot who took the high road to London, made vast numbers of them and his reputation spread all over Europe. He also made portrait medallions of more than 500 people, distinguished or obscure, and it is for these that he is most remembered. His work was carried on after his death in 1799 by his nephew William Tassie. James was the finer artist and some of his work is outstanding miniature sculpture. The Tassies made the portraits in a 'vitreous paste', which was really a kind of glass with a low melting point and which, when white, looked like marble.

James Tassie was born in Pollokshaws, then a village near Glasgow but now part of the city,* in 1735 and was apprenticed to a stone-mason. But on a public holiday he went to Glasgow and saw a collection of pictures owned by two brothers, Robert and Andrew Foulis, who also ran an academy of art at Glasgow University and ran a splendid printing press. He enrolled in the academy and studied there for three years and then went to Dublin to set up as a modeller and sculptor. There he met Dr Henry Quin, a professor of medicine, connoisseur,

---

*The Provost of Pollokshaws, at a ceremony to mark the amalgamation, took off his robes, laid them aside, and said: 'Here lie the abandoned habits of the last Provost of Pollokshaws.'

David Hume (*1711–1776*), *the most acute thinker in Britain during the eighteenth century. Adam Smith said that his friend approached as nearly as possible to the 'character of a perfectly wise and virtuous man as perhaps the nature of human frailty would permit'.*

Adam Smith—the only likeness of him to be done directly from the life.

James Tassie—modelled by his nephew William.

musician, and lover of the theatre. Quin was already making casts from engraved gems; he and Tassie evolved the vitreous paste. The recipe was secret and was lost when William Tassie died. But the glass was probably heated until it was pasty, pressed into a mould, and later polished. The casts reproduce detail with great accuracy.

The reproductions of engraved gems were treated to give different effects. They could be made transparent or opaque; tinted in various colours; given a 'layered' appearance like cameos.

Tassie went to London, on Quin's advice and with his help, in 1766. He set up in business and the early days there seem to have been hard. But he received an award of ten guineas from the Society for the encouragement of the Arts for 'Specimens of Profiles in Paste', exhibited his work at the Society of Artists and later at the Royal Academy, and gradually became known. The London jewellers set his gems in rings and other trinkets. He gradually built up a collection of moulds taken from gems in collections all over Europe, and his customers had a huge range of choice: nearly 16,000 different reproductions by 1791 and nearly 20,000 by the time of William's death.

An important event was an order in about 1783 from the Empress Catherine of Russia for a complete set of his gems—originally 10,000 but later added to. They were sent off in cabinets especially designed by James Wyatt R A, a fashionable and prolific architect.

A great catalogue of Tassie's stock was produced in 1791 by Rudolph Eric Raspe, Professor of Archaeology at Cassel and author of *The Adventures of Baron Munchausen*.

Tassie's skill is, however, best seen in his portrait medallions. A contemporary account said: 'He takes three sittings. The first two an hour each and the third not half an hour.' And: 'In taking likenesses he was, in general, uncommonly happy, and it is remarkable that he believed that there was a certain inspiration (like that mentioned by the Poets) necessary to give him full success ... He mentioned many instances in which he had been directed by it: and even some in which after he had laboured in vain to realise his ideas in wax, he had been able by a sudden flash of imagination to please himself in the likeness several days after he had last seen the original.'

He modelled the likeness first in red wax, using special small tools. From this moulds and casts had to be taken in plaster of Paris before the final product could be cast in the vitreous paste. The number of portraits sold depended on the fame of the sitter. Almost all are in profile, cut off just below the shoulder and some have the sitters name and the date. Most are about $1\frac{1}{2}$ inches (3.8 cm) high and are mounted on ovals about 4 inches (10 cm) by $3\frac{1}{2}$ inches (9 cm). A frame of boxwood was generally provided. A whole range of society is recorded; and among them is the only known authentic likeness of Adam Smith the economist.

James Tassie died in 1799. The *Glasgow Courier* said: 'Notwithstanding such elegant attainments, he seemed unconscious of merit, and, amidst the possession of foreign and domestic fame, he was modest, unassuming, and diffident. His private character was marked by the most amiable simplicity and inviolable integrity; by every quality which can recommend a man, and every virtue which can distinguish a Christian'.

William, who was born in 1777 and who had worked with James for several years, carried on the business, adding to the range. He was cultivated and well-travelled (James seems never to have gone abroad) and his studio became a meeting place for connoisseurs, artists, and poets (including Byron). Shelley wrote to Thomas Love Peacock, the poet and novelist, in 1822: 'I want you to do something for me; that is, to get me two pounds worth of Tassie's gems, the prettiest, according to your taste.'

William exhibited at the Royal Academy four times and issued three catalogues of his work. He retired in 1840 and died in 1860, bequeathing most of his stock in trade to the National Galleries of Scotland. This collection, now in the Scottish National Portrait Gallery, includes an almost complete set of the gems and a large number of portrait medallions. Collectors should beware of later plaster casts; but good reproductions in modern resins are available from the Scottish National Portrait Gallery.

Photographs

The geniuses Hill and Adamson

Scotland's contribution to civilisation has often been of a practical sort. Photography, a combination of art and science, was achieving great heights in Edinburgh during the 1840s within a very short time of its invention. The

David Octavius Hill (detail)

Robert Adamson (detail)

exponents were David Octavius Hill and Robert Adamson, whose partnership lasted only five years.

Hill (1802–1870) was the eighth child (as his middle name suggests) of a bookseller and publisher in Perth and he took up a career as an artist. Many of his paintings are typical of the era: castles, mountains, glens, all with an air of romance. He also illustrated books such as the novels of Scott and was a pioneer of lithography. He became secretary of the Royal Scottish Academy in 1830 and became an established and respected figure in Scottish art circles. Hill was secretary to the Academy for nearly 40 years—this, and his work as a painter, were remembered when he died, rather than his photography, for which he is now acclaimed.

His domestic life was rather unhappy. Only one of his children, Charlotte, survived infancy. She and his first wife Ann Macdonald, an amateur musician, died before he did; he then married Amelia Paton, a sculptress. He suffered from the effects of rheumatic fever for most of his adult life and for his last three years he was bedridden. But the *Scotsman* recorded: 'His manner in society was blithe and genial and he sang a capital song, not infrequently entertaining his companions with a ballad of his own composition.'

Adamson (1821–1848) was the son of a farmer. He wanted to become an engineer and started an apprenticeship but his health was poor. He was instead trained in photography by his brother, Dr John Adamson of St Andrews, and Robert set up a studio in Edinburgh probably in early 1843.

Hill and Adamson struck up a most fruitful partnership. It was, however, to last for a tragically short time, for Adamson died when he was 27, perhaps of consumption. A great national event was the catalyst in bringing their talents forward, as so often happens in the arts. This was the Disruption, a cataclysmic split in the Church of Scotland which resulted in the formation of the Free Church

The Scott Monument in Edinburgh in 1844 or 1845. A decision to build a monument to Sir Walter was taken almost immediately after his death in 1832 but the completion took 14 years.

of Scotland. The dispute was about how the Kirk was run, including the appointment of ministers. It came to a head in 1843 at the General Assembly of the Church, when about 200 ministers and elders walked out and formed their own assembly. It was for many of them a great sacrifice. Within a few days an Act of Separation and Deed of Demission were signed in Edinburgh in the presence of almost 500 people. Among them was Hill, and he decided to paint the scene. But such a task was enormous and he was used to landscapes rather than portraits. He was introduced to Adamson, who was already in business, and their great work began with photographs of a few of the participants to make things easier in painting the vast group. Much of their output is thus of dignitaries in the Free

Dr Robert Knox (1791–1862) who was one of the greatest teachers of anatomy of his day but who became involved in a particularly notorious scandal over murders. Medical men had difficulty in getting human bodies for teaching and research. The usual way was to buy bodies from people who robbed fresh graves. But William Burke, a vagrant, and William Hare, an Edinburgh lodging-house keeper, took to murder and sold the bodies. Knox bought some of them in 1828 and when the truth came out was mobbed, burnt in effigy, and in danger of violence. He seems to have taken too little care about how the bodies came to him. Hare turned King's evidence, Burke was hanged, and Knox afterwards had a chequered and disappointing career. Knox and his work were the subject of James Bridie's play, The Anatomist *(1930).*

Elizabeth Johnston, of Newhaven, whose work was to gut fish and carry them in a heavy creel on her back to sell them. She was a beauty but her hands show the harshness of her life. This is one of the most famous of Hill and Adamson works.

Church but they went in for much more than that. They did portraits of friends, relations, and notables, and their families.

They also produced marvellous studies of ordinary folk: stonemasons, soldiers, a blind harpist, and above all the fisher people of Newhaven, now part of Edinburgh—the men and their boats, the women who gutted and sold the fish, their children. The women's traditional striped dresses and the wickerwork of the creels came out well in the photographic medium that Hill and Adamson used. Fewer in number but excellent in quality are landscapes, for example of Edinburgh, St Andrews, and Durham. All the photographs capture the spirit of the age and yet have often a modern look. It was almost providential that during the very short time Hill and Adamson worked together the summers of 1846 and 1847 on the east coast were unusually sunny and dry: the best sort of weather for using cameras which had to have exposures of at least a minute compared with the split seconds of modern ones.

Some of the pictures were described as being 'executed by R. Adamson under the artistic direction of W. O. Hill'. The *Scotsman* said in 1870: 'Mr Hill's part was to see to the posing and grouping of the figures, the practical manipulation being conducted by Mr Adamson'. Little is in reality known about how the two worked together. Hill took up photography again long after Adamson's death. The results were poor for he tried to imitate paintings instead of using the medium as an art in its own right. This failure strongly suggests that Adamson was more than a technician.

Hill struggled on with painting the scene of the Disruption meeting and finished it 23 years after the great event. It is 5 feet (152 cm) by 11 feet 4 inches (334 cm) and has nearly 500 portraits. Many of them follow closely the 180 or more surviving photographs of ministers and of other people connected with the church. The painting was exhibited in Glasgow and Edinburgh, subscribers put up £1200 for its purchase, it was presented to the Free Church, and it is now in the Free Church's headquarters. Two of the figures are of poignant interest: Hill with pencil and pad and Adamson with a camera.

The two produced at least 1500 photographs. They are technically called calotypes, from the Greek *kalos* meaning beauty. The calotype process was patented in 1841 by William Henry Fox Talbot, an English squire and one of many inventors who contributed to the evolution of photography. It is a tribute to the genius of Hill and Adamson that they did their work at a time when the art and science of photography were in their infancy.

Charles Rennie Mackintosh

The Spook School

Glasgow was the centre of a notable movement in painting towards the end of the nineteenth century: the Glasgow Boys or the Glasgow School. It was also the cradle of a highly important movement in the decorative arts: the Glasgow Style,

The masterpiece of Charles Rennie Mackintosh—
The Glasgow School of Art.

which is bound up with the name of Charles Rennie Mackintosh (1868–1928).

Their achievements were great and spread the city's name. Yet no great school of artists has since then thrived in Glasgow; and Mackintosh was rejected by the Scottish establishment, did little in his later years, and took refuge in drink.

Mackintosh devised a style akin to Art Nouveau, the swirling, elongated, mannered style which started in Paris and was taken up, with variations, in almost every European country. His collaborators played a vital part: his friend Herbert MacNair (1868–1955) and the Macdonald sisters Margaret (1865–1933) and Frances (1874–1921). Mackintosh married Margaret and MacNair married Frances.

Mackintosh was apprenticed to an architect and his decorative work is almost inseparable from his architecture.

The 'Four' met at the Glasgow School of Art and did watercolours, illustrations, beaten metal work, leaded glass and posters. Swirling drapery, long slender figures, sinister or fairy-like imagery, and inspiration from Celtic myth all combined to give them the nickname the 'Spook School'.

Mackintosh's greatest piece of architecture is the building for the Glasgow School of Art: his firm won the competition for the design of the first part in 1896, and the conception was his. He also designed a few private houses, the Scotland Street School in Glasgow, a church, and in 1909—his last major commission in the city—the second part of the building for the School of Art. It is a triumph and yet was inexpensive to construct.

The Four had great successes with their work in exhibitions in Vienna, Turin, Paris, Rome, Munich, and elsewhere. Their fame was spread by articles in art magazines on the Continent as well as in Britain; yet they were ignored in London and found little encouragement in Glasgow. The style was either too advanced or was misunderstood.

One of his patrons, however, was Miss Cranston, who ran several tearooms in the city. For these rooms he did the whole interiors, dominated by chairs with extraordinarily high backs which are hardly designed for comfort. Some of the chairs are now decidedly ricketty—and not through age, for their construction was often slipshod.

Another great work was to design 'a room for a music lover', commissioned by a leading Austrian connoisseur. Mackintosh's influence on the Continent was enormous. But he was sensitive and not easy to work with; and he resigned his partnership in the architectural firm Honeyman and Keppie in 1914. Soon afterwards he left Glasgow for good. He lived in Chelsea from 1916 to 1923 and did practically no architectural work; but at the end of the First World War did some designs for textiles and turned increasingly to watercolours of landscapes and flowers.

He and his wife moved in 1923 to Port Vendres in the French side of the Pyrenées, quite poor. They returned to Britain in 1927 and Mackintosh died of cancer of the tongue in 1928.

Work by Mackintosh and the others of The Four comes on to the market in a steady trickle and is snapped up by collectors—Sotheby's branch in Belgravia,

London, sold work of theirs for more than £40,000 between 1971 and 1976. But furniture and other items influenced by their willowy and restrained version of art nouveau was made all over the country in watered-down versions

Balmorality

The Victorian view of Scotland

The love of Queen Victoria and Prince Albert for Scotland made the country and its style fashionable: tartans, deer stalking, 'pebble' jewellery, Scots baronial architecture, souvenirs of the Burns country, and, for the rich, owning an estate in the Highlands.

It all came about in curious ways. The royal pair visited Taymouth Castle in 1842 and the Prince wrote:

Scotland has made a most favourable impression on us both. The country is full of beauty, of a severe and grand character; perfect for sport of all kinds, and the air remarkably pure and light . . . The people are more natural, and are marked by that honesty and sympathy, which always distinguish the inhabitants of mountainous countries, who live far away from towns. There is, moreover, no country where historical traditions are preserved with such fidelity, or to the same extent. Every spot is connected with some interesting historical fact, and with most of these Sir Walter Scott's accurate descriptions have made us familiar.

The Queen's physician, Sir James Clark, believed in the health-giving properties of pure mountain air and recommended Deeside, near Aberdeen. They bought there the castle and estate of Balmoral. This was made possible by a bequest to the Queen of an immense fortune, thought to be about £500,000. It was from John Camden Neild (1780?–1852), a miser. His father, James, was a rich jeweller who did much good work in helping prisoners and pressing for reform of the prisons.

John Camden Neild wore shoes that were patched and down-at-heel; never allowed his clothes to be brushed because, he said, it harmed the cloth; never had an overcoat; and travelled by foot when possible to save expense. He spent the last 30 years of his life accumulating money. He did, however, have a considerable love and knowledge of literature.

Victoria said that Neild knew she would not squander his bequest. The little old castle of Balmoral was demolished and a larger one built. The Queen wrote in 1856: 'Every year my heart grows more fixed in this dear Paradise, and so much more now, that *all* has become my dearest Albert's *own* creation, own work, own building, own laying out . . . and his great taste, and the impress of his dear hand, have been stamped everywhere'. She wrote when she first saw Balmoral: 'It was so calm, and so solitary, it did one good as one gazed around; and the pure mountain air was most refreshing. All seemed to breathe freedom and peace, and to make one forget the world and its sad turmoils'.

Albert shot deer and Victoria sketched; they both went on long expeditions, sometimes riding and sometimes in carriages; one journey was of 129 miles in two days. Albert learned Gaelic and the Queen wrote: 'We were always in the habit of talking to the Highlanders—with whom one comes so much in contact in the Highlands. The Prince highly appreciated the good-breeding, simplicity, and intelligence, which makes it so pleasant, and even instructive to talk to them.'

The Queen also met here John Brown, a ghillie who became her most trusted servant and friend. Malicious gossip said that after Albert's death they married.

Two books by the Queen were immensely popular and helped to tell the world about the delights of Scotland; they are *Leaves from the Journal of Our Life in the Highlands* (published in 1868) and *More Leaves* (published in 1884). The first was dedicated to the memory of her husband and the second to the memory of John Brown. She achieved great success with her books. Income from them—*royalties*, in fact—amounted to more than £30,000. Disraeli, who wrote several best-selling novels and flattered her outrageously, said to her: 'We authors, Ma'am . . .' Others were not so kind. The Duchess of Cambridge said: 'Such bad vulgar English! So miserably futile & trivial! So dull and uninteresting!' Yet the Victorian view of Scotland has coloured what people think of that land now, and what the Scots think of themselves.

Balmoral Castle, Aberdeenshire, the romantic creation of Victoria and Albert.

Where to see Scottish Antiques

The great museums in the larger cities and towns have extensive collections which hardly need detailed explanation. Edinburgh, Glasgow, Aberdeen, and Dundee are especially rich.

Historic houses are mentioned below if they contain objects of specifically Scottish interest. But some historic houses are classic examples of international architecture and international art and antiques; this aspect of them has not been dealt with. Nor have museums and houses outside Scotland although many important and interesting objects are to be found in them.

Aberdeenshire

Braemar Castle: Jacobite relics, huge cairngorm, arms and armour.

Castle Fraser, Sauchen: furniture.

Craigievar Castle: locally made furniture.

Crathes Castle: seventeenth- and eighteenth-century furniture, painted ceilings.

Drum Castle: seventeenth-century oak cupboard.

Inverurie Carnegie Museum, Inverurie: arms, snuff mulls.

Peterhead Museum, St Peter Street, Peterhead: arms and snuff mulls.

Angus

Angus Folk Museum, Glamis: relics of everyday life, housed in six restored seventeenth-century cottages.

Glamis Castle: Jacobite relics and a fine collection of furniture, portraits, arms, textiles—but mostly not Scottish. A castle rich in historical associations.

Brechin Museum, Brechin: pewter communion plate, household goods, long case clocks, coins, tokens, fire arms, snuff boxes.

Forfar Folk Museum, Forfar: town regalia (chains of office etc.), silver, whaling weapons, weaving equipment, measures from gill to chopin.

Montrose Museum, Montrose: flintlock and percussion pistols, clocks, household items, polished agates, silver coins.

Signal Tower Museum, Arbroath: local craftsmen's equipment, household goods, glass bottles, communion tokens, snuff mulls, Arbroath silver.

Argyll

Duart Castle: brooches, dirks, pistols, snuff mulls.

Glencoe and North Lorn Folk Museum, Glencoe: weapons, bygones, items of horn, Jacobite and clan relics, snuff mulls, toys, costumes, farming tools.

Inverary Castle, Inverary: flintlock muskets, broadswords, targes and dirks, brooches, relics of Rob Roy, robes of the Order of the Thistle. The castle was severely damaged by fire in 1975, but restoration, a lengthy task, was quickly put in hand.

Public Library and Museum, Campbeltown: nineteenth-century domestic items, pistols.

Ayrshire

Bachelor's Club, Tarbolton: country furniture, Mauchline ware.

Carnegie Library, Museum, and Art Gallery, 12 Main Street, Ayr: Ayrshire embroidery.

Dick Institute, Kilmarnock: horn spoons and horn craft tools, Ayrshire needlework, printed calicoes including 'Paisley' shawls from Kilmarnock, machine lace, broadswords, engineering models, pottery, snuff mulls, long case clocks.

Souter Johnnie's Cottage, Kirkoswald: furniture for ordinary households.

Banff

Banff Museum: arms and armour.

Bute

Brodick Castle, Arran: a few items of silver.

Dumbartonshire

Cameron House, Alexandria: arms, relics of Tobias Smollett, the novelist.

Rossdhu, near Alexandria: furniture by Trotter of Edinburgh (about 1850), pewter communion set (1844), teapot by John Glen of Glasgow (about 1750).

Dumfriesshire

Carlyle's birthplace, Ecclefechan: country furniture.

Drumlanrig Castle: silver items made from silver mined in Scotland; tapestry panel worked by Mary Queen of Scots; barometer and long case clock; Jacobite relics, gilded and carved mirrors (Edinburgh, about 1770).

Dumfries Museum, The Observatory, Dumfries: firearms, furniture, pottery, clocks and clock faces, watches, Burns relics, coins, objects of everyday use.

Edinburgh

No. 7, Charlotte Square: the north side of the square, including no. 7, was designed by Robert Adam in 1791. No. 7 has been beautifully restored and refurnished in the Georgian style by the National Trust for Scotland. Scottish objects include furniture, a barometer, and kitchen utensils.

Palace of Holyrood House: broadswords of the sixteenth and seventeenth centuries, grates and firebaskets, furniture, relics of Mary Queen of Scots.

Elgin

Elgin Museum, 1 High Street, Elgin: Elgin silver, snuff mulls, pistols and other weapons, domestic items, Jacobite relics.

Fife

Falkland Palace, Falkland: early chairs, nineteenth-century reproductions of sixteenth-century chairs commissioned by the third Marquis of Bute.

Hill of Tarvit: early chairs for ordinary households, silver.

Museum and Art Gallery, Kirkcaldy: swords, dirks, cannons and cannon balls; long case clocks, watches; coins, medals, communion tokens, beggars' badges; costume, silver, much locally made pottery.

Scottish Fisheries Museum, St Ayles, Harbourhead, Anstruther: many items linked with fishing and seafaring.

Inverness-shire

Dunvegan Castle, Portree, Skye: 'Amen' glass given by the Young Pretender to Donald MacLeod of Galtrigal; relics of the Young Pretender and of Flora Macdonald.

Highland Folk Museum, Kingussie: objects in everyday use in the Highlands in former times, including costume, tartans, farming tools; reconstructed and furnished 'black house'.

Inverness Museum and Art Gallery, Castle Wynd, Inverness: silver from Inverness, Wick, and Tain; arms and armour; Jacobite relics; snuff mulls.

West Highland Museum, Cameron Square, Fort William: Jacobite relics, snuff mulls, tartan, armorial china, silver, arms, domestic objects, medals, regimental badges, maps and prints.

Kirkcudbrightshire

The Stewartry Museum, Kirkcudbright: domestic utensils, lace and embroidery, snuff boxes, the remarkable 'Siller' (or silver) Gun given to the burgh by James VI as a prize to encourage marksmanship, and the Silver Arrow made in 1838 to be competed for at the same time as the Siller Gun.

Lanarkshire

District Museum, Hamilton: pottery, treen, domestic, industrial and farming objects; vehicles.

Gladstone Court Museum, Biggar: reconstructed shops, workshops, schoolroom, photographer's studio, bank, and so forth . . . a delightful insight into the past.

Midlothian

Mallery House, Balerno: cabinet attributed to Deacon Brodie.

Orkney and Shetland

Tankerness House Museum, Kirkwall: communion tokens.

Peeblesshire

Traquair House, Innerleithen: the Bear Gates are said to have never been opened since the Young Pretender passed through them in 1745; nor will they be until the Stuarts are restored. Jacobite glass and miniatures, relics of Mary Queen of Scots, seventeenth-century carved oak, the cradle of James VI.

Perthshire

Blair Castle, Blair Atholl: exceptionally fine and extensive collection of Stuart and Jacobite relics. Quaichs, brooches, pistols, armorial porcelain, and a room furnished as the cottage of a well-to-do crofter of the eighteenth century.

Doune Castle, Doune: furniture.

Museum and Art Gallery, George Street, Perth: arms and armour, pottery and porcelain, snuff mulls, and an excellent collection of Perth silver from the late seventeenth century to the late nineteenth.

Scone Palace, Scone: bed hangings worked by Mary Queen of Scots; early nineteenth-century furniture.

Renfrewshire
Paisley Museum and Art Galleries, High Street, Paisley: paisley shawls.
Weaver's Cottage, Kalbarchan: eighteenth- and nineteenth-century furniture; general domestic items.

Ross and Cromarty
Hugh Miller's Cottage, Cromarty: furniture for an ordinary household.

Roxburgh
The Museum, Wilton Lodge, Hawick: silver, earthenware, communion and trade tokens.

Selkirk
Bowhill, near Selkirk: relics of Charles II's natural son the Duke of Monmouth, long case clocks by John Smith of Pittenweem, relics of Sir Walter Scott and of his friend James Hogg the poet, furniture, ram's head snuff mull, silver tankard (Edinburgh 1700).

Stirlingshire
Stirling Smith Art Gallery and Museum, Old High School, Academy Road, Stirling: pewter, pistols, snuff mulls, domestic objects, agricultural implements.

West Lothian
Hopetoun House, South Queensferry: designed by the Scottish architects Sir William Bruce and William, Robert, and John Adam. A noble mansion and a splendid collection but few specifically Scottish objects.
House of the Binns: furniture.
Kinneil Museum, Kinneil Estate, Bo'ness: Bo'ness pottery.

Military Museums
The Scottish United Services Museum, Edinburgh Castle, has the most extensive collection.

The more specialised regimental museums are: *Black Watch*, Perth; *Cameronians* (Scottish Rifles), Hamilton, Lanarkshire; *Gordon Highlanders*, Aberdeen; *King's Own Scottish Borderers*, Berwick on Tweed; *Royal Highland Fusiliers*, Glasgow; *Royal Scots*, Edinburgh Castle; *Queen's Own Highlanders (Seaforths and Camerons)*, Fort George, Inverness-shire; *Argyll and Sutherland Highlanders*, Stirling Castle.

Bibliography

Anglo-Saxon Chronicle, trans. by G N Garmonsway, Everyman Edition, J M Dent and Sons, London, 1953

Baker, Malcolm, 'Patrick Robertson's tea urn and the late eighteenth century Edinburgh silver trade', article in *Connoisseur*, London, August 1973

Bamford, Francis, 'The Rise and Decline of an Edinburgh Cabinet-maker', article in *Connoisseur*, London, August 1973

Bamford, Francis, article on 'Scottish furniture' in *Furniture History*, vol. ix 1973, Furniture History Society, London

Bamford, Francis, 'Some Edinburgh Furniture Makers', *Old Edinburgh Club Transactions* vol. xxxii

Bamford, Joan, 'Pebbles into Jewellery', article in *Art and Antiques Weekly*, London, 31 May 1975

Barker, T C, and Hatcher, John, *A History of British Pewter*, Longman, London, 1974

Beresiner, Yasha, and Narbeth, Colin, *The Story of Paper Money*, David and Charles, Newton Abbot, Devon, 1973

Blair, Claude, 'Scottish Firearms', article in *Bulletin of the American Society of Arms Collectors,* No. 31, Dallas, Texas, Spring 1975

Bradford, Ernle: *English Victorian Jewellery*, Country Life, London, 1959

Brook, A J S, 'Communion Tokens of the Established Church of Scotland', *Proceedings* of the Society of Antiquaries of Scotland, 13 May 1907, printed by Neil and Co., Edinburgh, 1908

Brown, P Hume, *Scotland, a Short History*, revised and enlarged edition, Oliver and Boyd, Edinburgh, 1961

Bryden, D J *Scottish Scientific Instrument Makers 1600–1900,* Royal Scottish Museum, Edinburgh, 1972

Bruce, David *Sun Pictures, the Hill-Adamson Calotypes*, Studio Vista, London, 1973

Buist, J S, 'Mauchline Ware', article in *Connoisseur*, London, August 1973

Burns, Robert, *The Poems and Songs* (Kinsley, James, editor), Clarendon Press, Oxford, 1968

Burns, Thomas *Old Scottish Communion Plate*, R and R Clark, Edinburgh, 1892

Chamberlain, G C, *The World of Coins*, Teach Yourself Books/Hodder and Stoughton, London 1976

Christie's, *Catalogues of Stuart Relics*, Christie, Manson and Woods, London, 20 February 1973 and 25 November 1975

Cochran-Patrick, R W, *Catalogue of the Medals of Scotland*, David Douglas, Edinburgh, 1884

Collier, W D, *The Scottish Regalia*, Her Majesty's Stationery Office, Edinburgh, 1970

Cripps, William Joseph, *Old English Plate,* 5th edition, John Murray, London, 1894

Daiches, David, *Charles Edward Stuart*, Thames and Hudson, London, 1973

Dick, Rev. Robert, *Scottish Communion Tokens other than those of the Established*

Church, Andrew Elliot, Edinburgh, 1902

Dictionary of National Biography (to 1900), Oxford University Press, London, reprinted edition, 1967–1968

Doud, Richard K: 'Scottish Cabinetmakers in Eighteenth-century America', *Scottish Art Review*, vol. xii, no. 1, 1969, published by the Glasgow Art Gallery and Museums Association

Douglas, James: *Scottish Banknotes*, Stanley Gibbons Publications, London, 1975

Drummond, James, *Ancient Scottish Weapons*, George Waterston and Sons, Edinburgh, 1881

Evans, Joan, *A History of Jewellery 1100–1870,* Faber and Faber, 2nd edition, 1970

Finlay, Ian, *The Scottish Tradition in Silver*, Saltire Society, Edinburgh, 1948

Finlay, Ian, *Scottish Crafts,* George G Harrap, London 1948

Finlay, Ian, *Scottish Gold and Silver Work*, Chatto and Windus, London 1956

Firsoff, V A, 'Scottish semi-precious stones', article in *Country Life*, 3 June 1971, London

Fleming, J Arnold, *Scottish Pottery*, first published by Maclehose, Jackson, Glasgow 1923 and reprinted with a new preface by Peter Walton, E P Publishing, Wakefield, Yorkshire, 1973

Flower, Margaret, *Victorian Jewellery*, Cassell, London, 1967

Fotheringham, Henry Steuart, 'Scottish Provincial Silver', *Antique Dealer and Collector's Guide*, August 1970, London

Fotheringham, Henry Steuart, 'More Notes on Scottish Silver', *Antique Dealer and Collector's Guide*, May 1972, London

Fotheringham, Henry Steuart, 'Scottish Silver Curiosities', *Antique Dealer and Collector's Guide*, February 1975, London

Garner, F H, and Archer, Michael, *English Delftware*, Faber and Faber, London, 1972

Gernsheim, Helmut, in association with Gernsheim, Alison, *The History of Photography*, Oxford University Press, London, 1955

Grant, Charles, *The Black Watch*, Osprey Publishing, Reading, Berkshire, 1973

Gray, John M, *James and William Tassie,* Walter Greenoak Patterson, Edinburgh, 1894

Hartman, George, 'Tobacconists' Figures', in *Antiques International* (Wilson, P C ed.), Michael Joseph, London, 1966

Hatcher, John, and Barker, T C, *A History of British Pewter*, Longman, London, 1976

Haynes, E Barrington, *Glass through the Ages*, Penguin, London, 1959

Henderson, James, 'Scottish Silver', article in *Antique Dealer and Collector's Guide*, August 1970, London

Hinks, Peter, *Nineteenth Century Jewellery*, Faber and Faber, London, 1975

Howard, David Sanctuary, *Chinese Armorial Porcelain*, Faber and Faber, London, 1974

Illustrated London News, unsigned article on 'Scottish pearl fishing', 14 September 1864

Jackson, Radwat, *English Pewter Touchmarks*, W Foulsham, London, 1970

Jones, George Hilton, *The Main Stream of Jacobitism*, Harvard University Press, Cambridge, Mass., 1954

Joslin E C, *The Standard Catalogue of British Orders, Decorations, and Medals (with valuations)*, Spink and Son, London, 3rd edition, 1976

Kelly, E M, *Spanish Dollars and Silver Tokens*, Spink and Son, London, 1976

Kirk, John L, *History of Firefighting*, pub. by Castle Museum, York, 1960

Knox, James, 'Scottish Snuff Mulls', article in *Antique Collector*, May 1975, London

Knox, James, 'Not to be sneezed at' (article on snuff mulls), *Country Life*, 23 September 1976, IPC Magazines, London, 1976

Mackenzie, Compton, *Sublime Tobacco,* Chatto and Windus, London

Maxwell, Stuart, 'The Highland Targe', *Scottish Art Review* vol. 9, no. 1, 1963, published by the Glasgow Art Gallery and Museums Association, Glasgow

Michaelis, Ronald, *Antique Pewter*, G Bell and Sons, London, 1955

Michaelis, Ronald, *British Pewter,* Ward Lock, London 1969

Narbeth, Colin, *How to Collect Paper Money,* Arthur Barker, London, 1971

National Museum of Antiquities of Scotland, *Brooches in Scotland* (no author given), NMAS, Edinburgh, 1971

Neal, W Keith, and Back, D H L, *Forsyth & Co Patent Gunmakers*, G Bell and Sons, London 1969

Nimlin, Jock, *Let's Look at Scottish Gemstones,* Jarrold and Sons, Norwich, in association with the National Trust for Scotland, no date

O'Day, Deirdre, *Victorian Jewellery*, Letts, London, 1974

Ovenden, Graham (ed), *Hill and Adamson Photographs* (with an introduction by Henderson, Marina), Academy Editions, London, and St Martin's Press, New York, 1973

Paton, James (ed), *Scottish History and Life*, James Maclehose, Glasgow, 1902

Patterson, Jerry E, *A Collector's Guide to Relics and Memorabilia*, Crown Publishers, New York, 1974

Paul, I, *The Scottish Tradition in Pottery*, Saltire Society, Edinburgh, 1948

Peter, Mary *Collecting Victorian Jewellery,* MacGibbon and Kee, London, 1970

Pinto, E H, *Wooden Bygones of Smoking and Snuff Taking,* Hutchinson, London, 1961

Pinto, E H, *Treen and Other Wooden Bygones,* G Bell and Son, London 1969

Pinto, E H and Eva, *Tunbridge and Scottish Souvenir Woodware,* G Bell and Sons, London, 1970

Peal, Christopher, *British Pewter*, John Gifford, London, 1971

Petrie, Sir Charles, *The Jacobite Movement*, Eyre and Spottiswoode, London, 1959

Purves, Alec A, *Collecting Medals and Decorations*, B A Seaby, London, revised edition, 1971

Purvey, P Frank, *Coins and Tokens of Scotland* (Part 4 of Seaby's *Standard Catalogue of British Coins*), B A Seaby, London 1972

Reid, Alexander John Forsyth, *The Reverend Alexander John Forsyth . . . and his invention of the percussion lock*, Aberdeen University Press, Aberdeen, 1909

Rogers, Tom, and de Rin, Victoria, 'Wemyss Ware', article in *Antique Dealer and Collector's Guide*, London, November 1976

Scott, Amoret and Christopher, *Discovering Staffordshire Figures,* Shire Publications, Tring, Hertfordshire, 1969

Scott, Sir Walter, *The Fortunes of Nigel,* Everyman Edition, Dent, London, 1965

Scottish National Portrait Gallery, *James and William Tassie,* leaflet, no author and no date, Edinburgh

Smith, John, *Old Scottish Clockmakers,* Oliver and Boyd, Edinburgh, second edition 1921

Smout, T C, *A History of the Scottish People 1560–1830,* Collins, London, 1969

Spink and Son, *Catalogue of Dundee Collection of Scottish Coins sold in Los Angeles, Calif., 19 February 1976,* Spink and Son, London, and Bowers and Ruddy Galleries, Los Angeles

Stewart, Ian Halley, *The Scottish Coinage,* 2nd edition, Spink and Son, London 1967

Victoria, Queen, *Leaves from the Journal of Our Life in the Highlands,* Folio Society, London, 1973

Wallace, John, *Scottish Swords and Dirks,* Arms and Armour Press, London, 1970

White, Joy Scott, Scottish Georgian silver spoons, *Antique Collector,* August 1969, London

Whiting, J R S, *Trade Tokens, a Social and Economic History,* David and Charles, Newton Abbot, Devon, 1971

Wilkinson, Wynard R T, *Indian Colonial Silver,* Argent Press, London, 1973

Wilkinson, Wynard R T, *A History of Hallmarks,* Queen Anne Press, London, 1975

Wood, L Ingleby, *Scottish Pewterware and Pewterers,* George A Morton, Edinburgh, 1904

INDEX

Illustrations are indicated by italicised figures.